933.
3332.

THE TALE OF ANCIENT ISRAEL

DEDICATED TO

HUGH AND CELIA TOUSSAINT

*In memory of our visits to the scenes of this book
in
Egypt, Mesopotamia and Palestine*

Abraham and Isaac. (*See page 38*)

THE TALE OF ANCIENT ISRAEL

RETOLD BY
ROGER LANCELYN GREEN

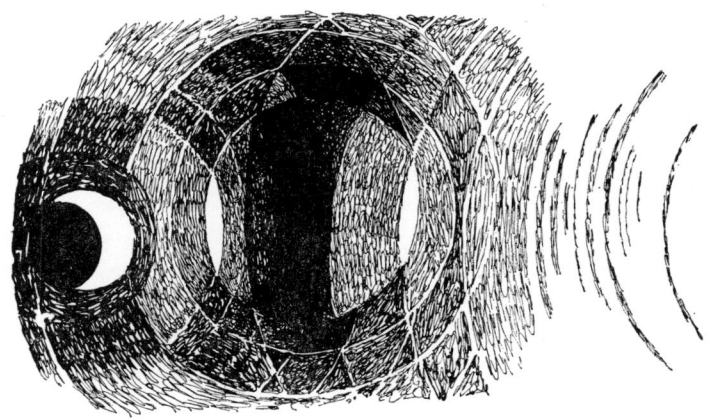

Illustrated by CHARLES KEEPING

LONDON: J. M. DENT & SONS LTD
NEW YORK: E. P. DUTTON & CO. INC.

ROGER LANCELYN GREEN was born on 2nd November 1918 at Norwich, but has spent most of his life at Poulton-Lancelyn in Cheshire, where his ancestors have been Lords of the Manor for thirty generations. He spent most of his childhood at home, owing to ill health, but in 1937 entered Merton College, Oxford, where he took an honours degree in English Language and Literature, followed by the post-graduate degree of Bachelor of Letters, and later was Deputy Librarian of the college for five years. He has also been a professional actor, an antiquarian bookseller, a schoolmaster and a Research Fellow at Liverpool University for short periods. Since 1950 he has lived at Poulton-Lancelyn and devoted most of his time to writing.

Besides scholarly works on Andrew Lang, Lewis Carroll, A. E. W. Mason, J. M. Barrie and others, he has written many books for young readers. These include adventure stories such as 'The Theft of the Golden Cat' (1955), fairy-tale fantasies such as 'The Land of the Lord High Tiger' (1958), and romances set in Greece of the legendary period such as 'Mystery at Mycenae' (1957) and 'The Luck of Troy' (1961). But he is best known for his retelling of the old myths and legends, from 'King Arthur' (1953) and 'Robin Hood' (1956) to 'Heroes of Greece and Troy' (1960) and 'Myths of the Norsemen' (1962). He has visited Egypt once and Greece many times, and has written about them for young readers, telling of their history as well as of their legends—his own favourites being 'Old Greek Fairy Tales' (1958), his adventure story set in ancient Greece, Scandinavia and Britain 'The Land Beyond the North' (1958), 'Ancient Egypt' (1963) and 'A Book of Myths' (1965).

© Text, Roger Lancelyn Green, 1969. © Illustrations, J. M. Dent & Sons Ltd, 1969. All rights reserved. Text printed by the Aldine Press, Letchworth, Herts, colour plates printed by Lowe & Brydone (Printers) Ltd, London, for J. M. Dent & Sons Ltd, Aldine House, Bedford Street, London. First published 1969.

SBN: 460 05079 6

CONTENTS

INTRODUCTION   xi

I. THE GREAT MYTHS
In the Beginning   3
The Great Flood   12
The Tower of Babel   18

II. THE FAMILY OF ISRAEL
The Adventures of Abraham   25
Isaac and Rebekah   37
Esau and Jacob   44
Joseph and His Brothers   56
Israel in Egypt   71

III. THE ESCAPE OUT OF EGYPT
The Adventures of Moses   79
The Ten Plagues   87
The Downfall of Pharaoh   97
Through the Wilderness   101

IV. THE PROMISED LAND
The Fall of Jericho   115
'The Sword of the Lord and of Gideon'   124
Samson and the Philistines   133
The Story of Ruth   147

V. DAVID, KING OF ISRAEL

Samuel the Prophet 153
The Boy David 163
The Witch of En-Dor 173

ILLUSTRATIONS

COLOUR

Abraham and Isaac	*frontispiece*
	facing page
Adam and Eve	4
The Egyptians in the Red Sea	83
The priests blew their trumpets	98

BLACK AND WHITE

War in Heaven	7
. . . the rain fell, and the Ark floated higher and higher	16
Higher still grew the tower	20
. . . he could see the flare of burning Sodom	35
Isaac blessed Esau and Jacob	54
They threw him into the pit	58
They set out on the long trek into Egypt	72
The Messenger spoke out of the burning bush, saying, 'Moses! Moses!'	84
All the beasts sickened with the cattle plague	92
For forty years the Israelites wandered through the wilderness	110
They shouted with a great shrill cry	120
There lay Sisera dead with the tent peg driven through his head	127
His daughter came dancing out to meet him	135
. . . crying, 'Death to my enemies—and to me!' Samson strained forward with all his might	145
Goliath rushed forward, mad with rage	168

MAPS

The wanderings of the Children of Israel	viii
Egypt and Babylonia, 2000–1500 B.C.	x

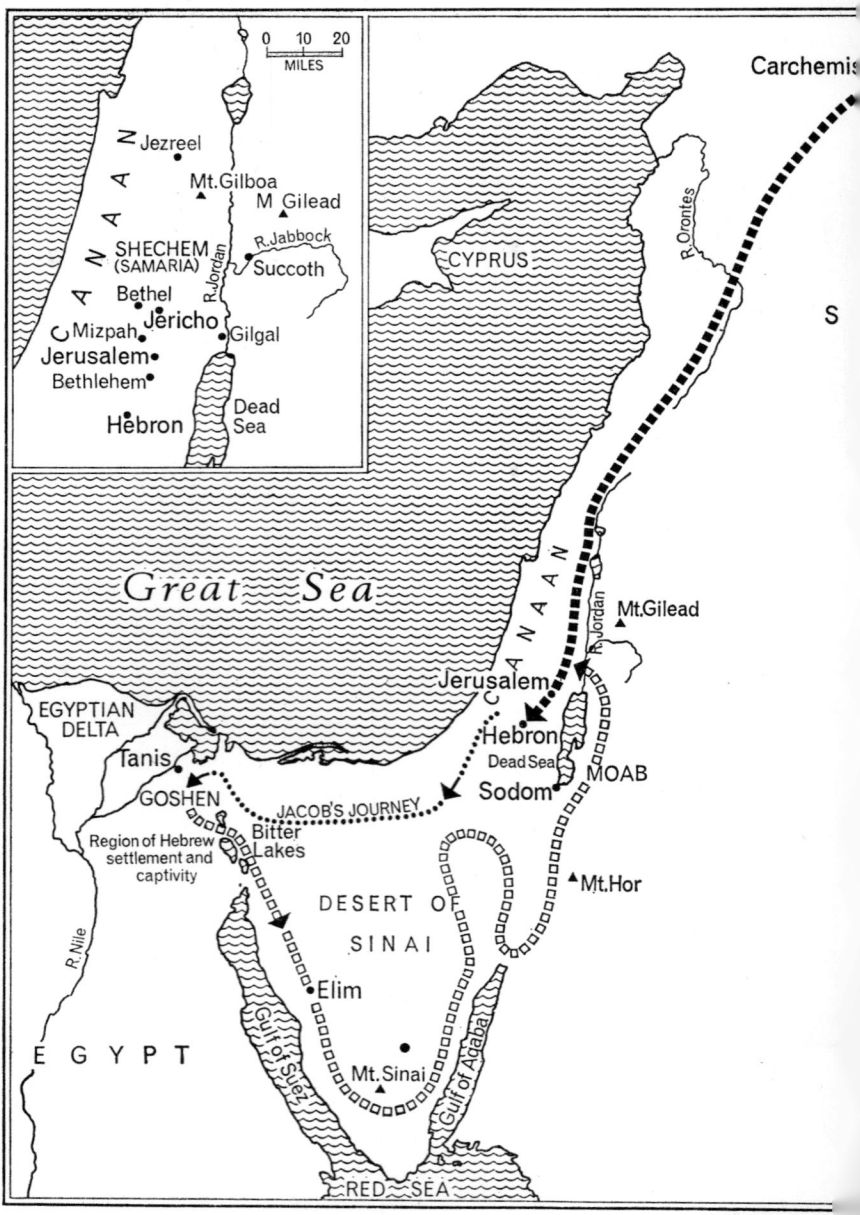

The wanderings of the Children of Israel

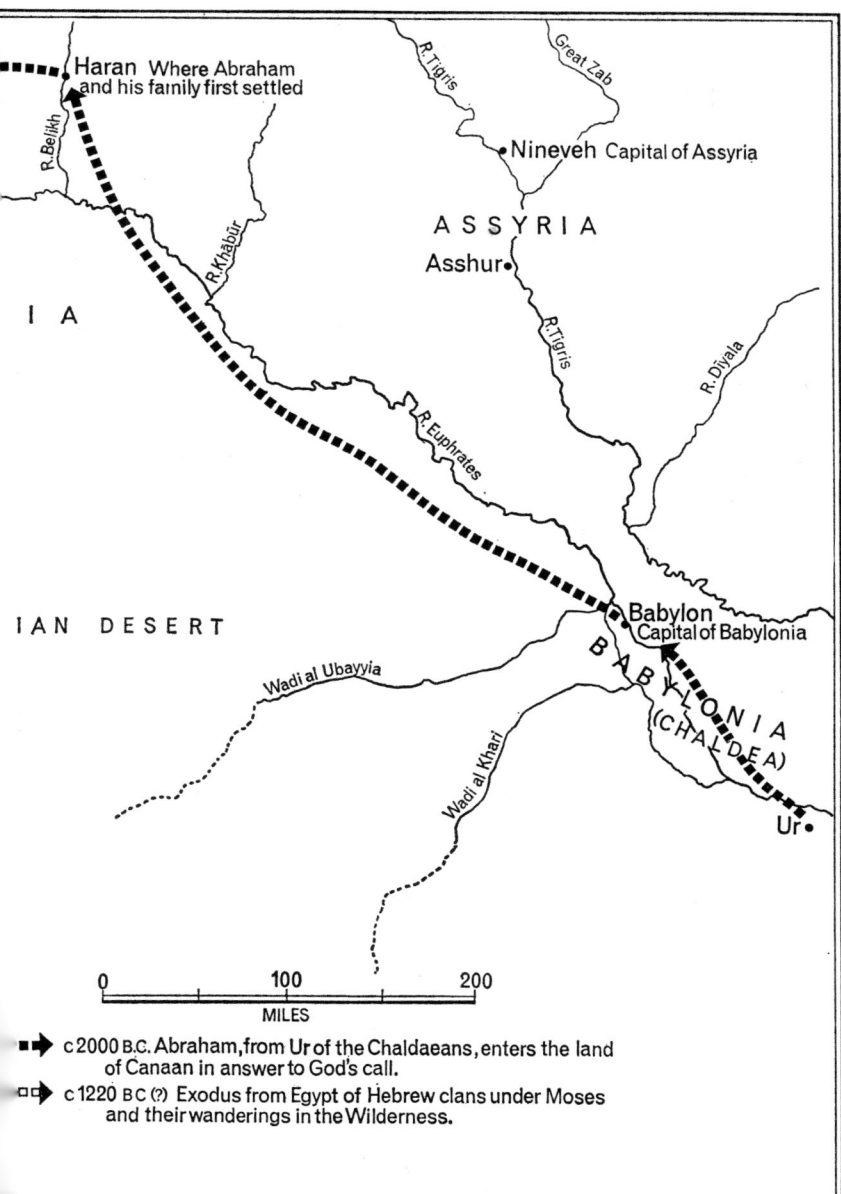

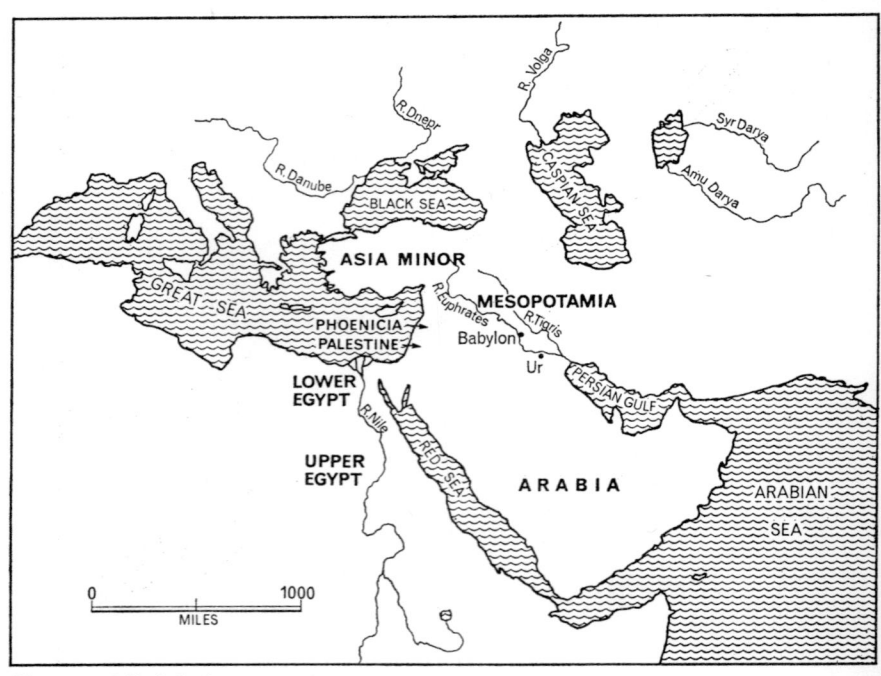

Egypt and Babylonia, 2000–1500 B.C.

INTRODUCTION

IN A sense all myths are true—though some myths are truer than others—for a myth tries to describe in the form of a story something real, but outside the myth maker's understanding or beyond his powers of accurate description.

We are still making myths; for while we can all describe time as we know it in our lives and surroundings, even the scientists have to make a myth to describe eternity; we can describe a measurable space of ground, but we need a myth to describe outer space. We may call time or space a circle; but that is only a myth made because we cannot imagine endless time or endless space in any other way.

Ever since men and women could think they have been making up myths; and the more clearly and reasonably they are able to think the more convincing do their myths become. The first Red Indian tribes said that a musk rat fished up some soil out of the deep waters and made it into the earth; the ancient Egyptians brought Ra the sun-god like a golden egg out of the same deep waters to create the world; the ancient Greeks told of the marriage of Uranus and Gaea—sky and earth—from whom were born the elder gods who then proceeded with the work of creation, as Ra had done in Egypt; the Babylonians married Apsu and Tiamat—fresh water and salt water—to be the parents of the gods, and so on.

Just in the same way the people of Israel made their myths, telling of how Jahveh created the world and set the first man and woman in the Garden of Eden. And they went on to tell of the Flood which Noah survived in the Ark, as Ziusudra did in ancient Babylonian myth and Deucalion in the Greek story.

The Israelites had far fewer myths in the strict sense than most of the other nations of the ancient world, but they had at least as many miraculous legends—histories of actual events so twisted and glorified in the telling that the result is a mixture of fact and fiction that can hardly be disentangled.

After the myths in Book One the stories in this book are the legends of ancient Israel: the history of their adventures in Egypt and their return to and conquest of Palestine as the stories of these two events grew and developed in the telling until they became legends—just as the true stories of the Mycenean age and of the siege and fall of Troy were turned by the Greeks into the great heroic legends told by Homer and the other poets of Hellas and Ionia. The Egyptian story of the 'Exodus' was very different from the Israelite version of the same historical event.

The Jewish story of the creation may be a myth, and Moses or Samson or David no more nor less historical characters than Theseus or Heracles or Achilles, but there is one great difference between the myths and legends of Israel and those of Egypt or Babylon or Greece.

At the back of all the myths of all peoples, from the Bushmen of central Africa to the most sophisticated Greeks, there is the dim knowledge that 'in the beginning God created the heaven and the earth'. Indeed that is what all myths of the creation are trying to say, in whatever form they may picture God, and in whatever way they try to describe what the actual making of the world, of nature and of mankind was like.

Of course we cannot possibly know what God is like, or how the creation took place, or imagine what the after-life—Heaven or Hell—will be like. We can only make up myths, based on what we know and see and feel in this world: describing the golden floors of Heaven, because gold is the richest and purest of earthly metals; or the fires of Hell, because burning is the most agonizing physical pain that we can imagine. But we know that both are myths—reflections in an earthly mirror of something that earthly eyes cannot see: that Heaven is a spiritual union with God and Hell the horror of spiritual exile from Him. . . .

Into this strange mixture of ignorance and understanding came the point where Time and Eternity crossed (the very metaphor is itself another myth), and God became Man in the person of Jesus Christ.

This book has nothing to do with religion in that higher sense. But the point is that Christ had to be born as a man in some country and as a member of some human race. For this reason there had to be a Chosen People—and that people was Israel.

'How odd of God to choose the Jews!' says the well-known quip—but the reason is quite obvious. The Israelites were the one race in antiquity who—in spite of many back-slidings— firmly and continuously for well over a thousand years worshipped one God and tried to follow the strictest code of rules, which we still accept as the Ten Commandments.

Egypt came nearest to deserving the choice; for while the Israelites were still wandering in the wilderness the Pharaoh Akhenaten (1370–1352 B.C.) tried for his brief, tragic reign to overthrow the numerous gods and superstitions of Egypt and lead his people into the knowledge and worship of one God, whom he called Aten and whose visible reflection—*not* God himself— was the sun.

Akhenaten failed and perished miserably, while Egypt lapsed into even deeper polytheism—worship of even more gods than before. Greece might have achieved the knowledge of the truth to which poets like Aeschylus and thinkers like Socrates drew so near—but was led astray by giving undue importance to politics and philosophy and a mild polytheism that accepted all gods and all faiths, in which the Romans followed her.

And so the Israelites became the Chosen People rather than the much pleasanter and more civilized Egyptians and Greeks. In a cruel world they seem to have been the cruellest—though we must remember the piles of heads of slaughtered enemies in the sculptures celebrating the victories of Rameses the Great of Egypt (some two hundred years before David came to the throne of Israel), or the cold-blooded massacre of the male inhabitants of Melos by the Greeks during a period of mob rule at Athens five hundred years after him.

It was the religious fervour which made the Israelites outstanding in the ancient world, and for this purity of faith and their high ideals of life and conduct much must be forgiven—and much was forgiven. For however definitely 'chosen', we must never forget that the Israelites were ordinary human beings of their period. Moreover the knowledge that they were 'chosen' seems to have gone to their heads, as power of any sort does, and we must understand and excuse much of their intolerance and pride.

This must seem a much too serious Introduction to a storybook; but it is necessary to explain why the myths of ancient Israel are of all myths those that come nearest to the truth; and why the history of the Israelites, however legendary, has always been treated as of so much more importance than the legends of any other race.

But once this has been said, here are some of the best and certainly some of the most famous stories in the world—and stories that I have tried to retell simply for their own sake as if they had been the myths and legends of any other people—just as I have already retold so many other stories of the ancient world, of the Greeks, of the Egyptians, and of all those included in *A Book of Myths*, to which this is a companion volume.

Book One

THE GREAT MYTHS

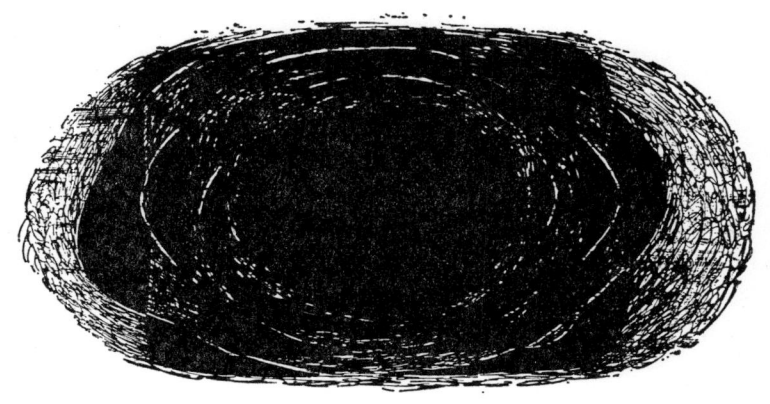

IN THE BEGINNING

In the beginning Jahveh made both the earth and the sky. At first the earth was unformed, and it was mingled with the sea in the darkness. But Jahveh said, 'Let there be light'—and at once there was light.

Jahveh looked upon the light and saw that it was good, and said: 'This I call Day—and it is day. As for the darkness, that I call Night—and it is night. Now here are the evening and the morning of the First Day of the world.'

Then Jahveh said: 'Let there be a great space above the earth, and let it hold back that out of which the world was made.'

At once it was even as Jahveh commanded; and he looked upon it, saw that it was good, and said: 'This is the Sky—and it *is* the sky. And now come the evening and the morning of the Second Day of the making of the world.'

Next Jahveh said: 'Let the waters be gathered together, and the dry land rise up through them.' At once it was even as he commanded, and he went on to name them, saying: 'These are Sea and Earth—and they are so. But they are not yet complete. Let the earth bring forth grass and trees, bearing seeds from which more trees and grass may grow.'

At once all happened as Jahveh willed, and he looked upon what he had made and saw that it was good—and the evening and the morning of their making were the Third Day.

Then Jahveh said: 'Let there be lights in the sky to divide the day from the night; and from their changing let years and days come, and seasons also.' So Jahveh made two great lights; the greater light he called the Sun—and it was the sun—and he set it to rule the day. He made a lesser light also to rule the night, calling it the Moon—and it was the moon; and he made the stars also. And when he had made all these and set them in the sky he looked upon them and saw that they were good—a good work for the Fourth Day.

For the Fifth Day, Jahveh said: 'Let there be living creatures in the waters and in the air.' And at once there were whales and every other kind of fish in the sea; and above it flew all manner of birds and other winged creatures. And Jahveh looked upon them and saw that they were good.

Then Jahveh said: 'Let the earth bring forth all kinds of living creatures, both four-footed and creeping things.' And at once all manner of animals and insects came out of the ground, each of its own kind, and Jahveh looked upon them and saw that they were good.

And he said: 'Now I will make Man in my own likeness, to be an image of me, and he and his descendants shall rule over all created things—over the fish of the sea and the birds of the air and the beasts of the field, over all the earth and over everything that creeps upon it.'

So Jahveh made Man in his own likeness. And he said to all the creatures which he had made:

'Live and be fruitful: eat of the herbs and of the fruits that I have made for you.' Then Jahveh looked upon all that he had made and saw that it was good. And this was the evening and the morning of the Sixth Day.

Now Jahveh rested from his great work of creation, and he said: 'On this the Seventh Day of the Making of the World I have rested. For ever afterwards I make each seventh day holy:

Adam and Eve. (*See page 6*)

let all rest upon that day and be grateful to me for this my work of creation, and worship me.'

Although the world was made, it was still wild. But presently Jahveh sent a mist over it to water the ground. Where the mist had been he planted a garden, away to the east, and called it Eden. And in Eden he planted all those trees and flowers that are pleasant to the sight and bear fruits that are good for food. But he also planted there two magic trees: the Tree of Life and the Tree of the Knowledge of Good and Evil.

And a river went out of Eden, after it had watered the garden, and was divided into four great rivers to water the whole earth. And these were the Pison, which we now call the Ganges, that waters the land of Havilah (India), rich in gold and precious stones; the Gihon (the Nile), which passes through the lands of Ethiopia and Egypt; and the Tigris and Euphrates, which flow to the east of Assyria.

When Eden was prepared, Jahveh took Adam, the First Man—breathing into him a living soul—and set him to tend the garden and to dwell there in perfect happiness.

And he said to Adam: 'Your joy shall be to tend my garden; and all that is in it is yours, and you may freely eat of the fruits that grow there. But I lay one command upon you: do not eat the fruit of the Tree of Knowledge, for if you do you will bring Sin and Death into the world—things of which as yet you know nothing.'

So Adam dwelt in the Garden of Eden, and tended it. And all the animals and other wild creatures were tame and friendly; and he gave them their names, and to all the trees and flowers also.

But Jahveh said: 'It is not good that Adam should dwell here alone, without another of his own kind. I will make him a companion to help in all that he does.'

Then Jahveh sent a deep sleep upon Adam. And when he woke there stood beside him a beautiful woman; and it seemed to Adam that while he slept Jahveh had taken a rib from his side and made this woman to be his wife.

And Adam said: 'This woman is bone of my bone and flesh of my flesh: for ever after a man shall leave his father and mother and shall dwell with his wife and love her only: for they shall be one flesh.'

After this Adam and his wife Eve lived in the Garden of Eden in perfect happiness and perfect innocence. They walked naked together among the wild creatures, knowing no fear nor shame; suffering no hardship, wishing for nothing which had not been given to them, lord and lady of all things yet worshipping Jahveh in joy and delight, and, in token of their service to their Maker, obeying his one command—that they should not eat of the fruit of the Tree of Knowledge.

Yet Paradise was not to last for ever. Adam and Eve had been given freedom of choice with the souls that were breathed into them; and their Maker intended wonders and tribulations for them and for their descendants that would have been without meaning if they had been mere walking images with no choice between good and evil.

Before the world was made, somewhere beyond time and outside human understanding, one of the spirits who served Jahveh—a messenger or angel whose dwelling was in Heaven—had disobeyed, since he too had free will. His sin was pride, for he set himself up as an equal to his Maker, and was cast out of Heaven with others of the angels who chose to follow his evil lead. And Michael, the leader of the faithful angels, drove him with his flaming sword down into the darkness that is outside the light of Heaven, and into the fires that must burn all those who are separated from the Creator.

This evil angel who, when he became a devil, was called Satan —'the Adversary'—stole into Eden and somehow persuaded the serpent to let him enter into and possess him.

And the serpent seemed no different from his usual self as he came through the garden and met Eve one day when she was tending the flowers not far from the Tree of Knowledge.

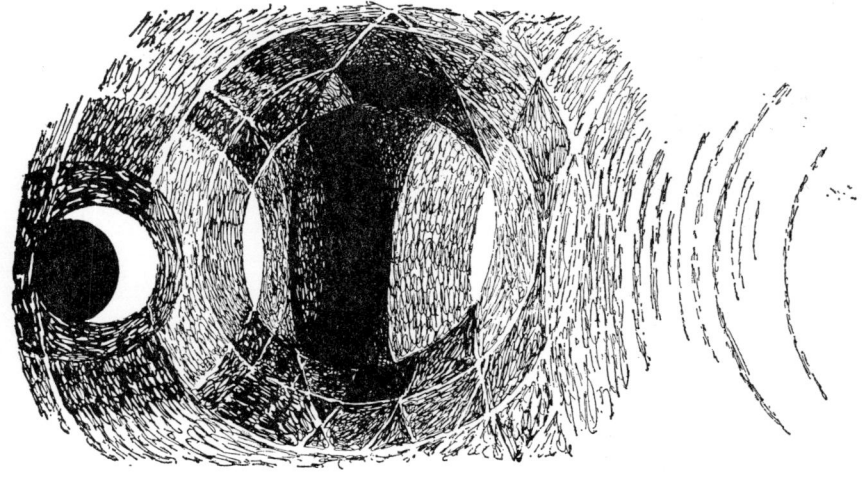

War in Heaven

They spoke together, as in those days all living creatures could, and presently the serpent said:

'And so Jahveh has indeed told you that you may eat any fruit from any tree in the garden?'

Eve answered: 'Yes, we may eat the fruit of any tree—except for the one which stands in the middle of Eden and is called the Tree of Knowledge. Jahveh has said that we must not eat the fruit of that one tree, for if we do we shall die.'

'It is not that you will die if you eat it,' said the serpent, 'but that you will cease to be mere creatures such as we all are. Instead, if you eat that fruit, you and Adam will become wise, just as Jahveh is. Yes, you will know all that he knows—you will, for a start, know what Good and Evil are. These are but words with which Jahveh has tried to frighten you. Do you not want to know and to feel these new and wonderful things?'

So the serpent went on persuading and tempting Eve until in her curiosity to taste the magic fruit she forgot the one easy command which Jahveh had laid on her and Adam, the one token of their obedience. So she plucked the fruit of the Tree of Knowledge and, finding it delicious, took it to Adam and persuaded him to eat it also.

A little while after they had eaten the fruit a change came upon Adam and Eve. They knew that they had disobeyed Jahveh, and so they knew Sin for the first time, and were open to all manner of temptations and thoughts of evil which had never entered their heads before.

Yet with the thoughts of Evil came also the Knowledge of Good; and with temptation the urge to fight against it in all its forms. And to begin with, for they now for the first time felt ashamed of being naked, they plucked fig-leaves and wove them together to make short kilts.

They had scarcely done this when they heard the voice of Jahveh calling them in the wind that went through the garden in the cool of the day—and they hid themselves among the trees.

But Jahveh called again, saying: 'Adam, where are you?'

Then Adam answered: 'I heard your voice in the garden, and I was afraid because I was naked, and so I hid myself.'

'Who told you that you were naked?' came the voice of Jahveh. 'Answer: have you eaten the fruit of the tree that I commanded you not to touch?'

'It was the woman whom you gave me to be my wife who brought me the fruit and persuaded me to eat,' answered Adam.

'The serpent cheated and deceived me into eating the fruit,' Eve hastened to explain.

Then said Jahveh: 'Serpent, because of what you have done, you shall be the most hated of all creatures. Woman, because of what you have done, you must now bear children in pain and danger, and to remind you of your disobedience you and your daughters for ever shall be subject to your husbands. As for you, Adam, because you have listened to the tempting words of your wife and eaten the fruit which I commanded you not to touch, the ground shall no longer bring forth all that you need. From now on thorns and thistles shall spring up beneath your feet, and you must clear the weeds and brambles, dig the soil, sow and tend your crops and thus gain your living by the sweat of your brow. And when your life on earth is ended your body shall return into the earth: for dust you are and to dust you shall return. Moreover, lest with your new knowledge and your new weakness you should be tempted to eat the fruit of the Tree of Life and live for ever, I will send you out of Paradise to till the ground from which you were taken.'

And so Adam and Eve were driven out of the Garden of Eden, into the wilderness outside. And Jahveh set an angel with a flaming sword at the eastern gateway of the Garden of Eden so that they could not go back into it ever again.

Yet although Paradise was lost to them because of their disobedience, Adam and Eve did not fare too badly in their new home on the outskirts of Eden. For Adam soon learned to till the ground and grow corn; to herd sheep and cattle, and to protect them against the wild beasts who now sought to prey on them. And Eve learned to spin and weave, to sew skins together, and to grind the corn and bake bread for her family.

For very soon after they had left Eden children began to be born to them; and the eldest of these were two sons called Cain and Abel.

As he grew up Abel learned to be a shepherd—tending and feeding the flocks of sheep which gave them meat for food, and milk to make into cheese, and wool for Eve and her daughters to weave into garments.

But Cain became a farmer, tilling the soil and harvesting his corn to be ground into flour for bread.

Although they dwelt no longer in Eden, Adam and Eve taught their children to worship and make sacrifices to Jahveh and keep holy each seventh day in honour of the Maker of all things. And at special times special festivals were held, in particular at the end of harvest in thankfulness for the stores of corn and the growing lambs which would keep starvation away during the winter.

One harvest festival Cain and Abel brought their offerings as sacrifices to Jahveh in their usual way. Abel brought the best of his lambs and offered them up to Jahveh with a glad and thankful heart—and Jahveh received the offering in the spirit in which it was made.

But Cain brought his offerings of corn and fruit grudgingly, as a duty rather than with any feeling of thankfulness—and Jahveh would not accept them.

Then Cain flew into a violent rage, and he clenched his fists and ground his teeth, and grew pale with fury.

Then Jahveh said to Cain: 'Why are you so angry, and for what reason do you glare so? If you did well, your sacrifice would be accepted; but offering it as you do, you commit sin rather than perform an act of worship. If you made your offerings in the same spirit as Abel does, you would be preferred to him—but as it is, he is better than you.'

Cain said nothing. But the evil sin of jealousy woke in his heart, and he began to hate his brother Abel. And one day when they were alone in the fields they fell into an argument, and Cain struck Abel on the head with his hoe and killed him.

When he saw Abel's blood staining the ground, and Abel's body lying still and lifeless, Cain was filled with fear and tried to run away and hide among the trees.

But Jahveh who sees all spoke to him, saying: 'Cain, Cain! Where is your brother Abel?'

And Cain answered with a lie, saying: 'I do not know where Abel is. Why should I? Am I my brother's keeper?'

But Jahveh could not be deceived and spoke to Cain, saying: 'What have you done? The voice of your brother's blood calls to me from the ground, and now there is a curse upon you and upon the earth—you who have shed man's blood for the first time. From now on you shall be an outcast and a wanderer, and your home shall be in the desert.'

Then Cain wept and cried: 'My punishment is greater than I bear. I must wander alone for the rest of my days, since every man's hand will be raised against me to slay me as I slew Abel.'

But Jahveh placed a mark on Cain so that all men might know him, and he said: 'Whoever slays Cain shall suffer vengeance.'

Then Cain made his home in the land of Nod on the east side

of Eden; and he lived to see his grandchildren, and their grandchildren's children—for in the days before the Flood men lived for many hundreds of years.

Yet one of them slew him in the end. His name was Lamech, and when he was old and his eyes were dim, he took his bow in hand and went out hunting with his little son Tubal-Cain, the child of his old age.

Presently Tubal-Cain saw something move behind the bushes, and he said to his father:

'Look! There is a wild beast moving over there! I can see his shaggy fur!'

Quickly Lamech fitted an arrow to the string and loosed strongly towards the shaking bushes which he could only dimly see, and struck his mark.

But when they went to look at what he had slain, Lamech found that it was Cain, clad in the rough skin which he had worn ever since he became an outcast.

So Cain died a violent death, at the hands of a kinsman, even as Abel had died. But Lamech wept and lamented, fearing the wrath of Jahveh. Yet as he had killed Cain in ignorance, the vengeance did not fall upon him.

But some say that when he became quite blind he killed his own son Tubal-Cain with a blow of his fist, not knowing where he struck—and the sorrow for the loss of his son was a harder punishment than death itself.

THE GREAT FLOOD

ADAM and Eve had many other children besides Cain and Abel, and the earth was peopled by their sons and daughters, and the race of men grew and multiplied for almost two thousand years.

They were mighty men in those days and lived to great ages: Adam himself lived for nine hundred and thirty years, and one of his descendants called Methuselah died at the age of nine hundred and sixty-nine.

But as men and women grew more and more numerous upon the face of the earth, they grew more wicked also. And certain of the evil angels who had been cast out of Heaven with Satan came to dwell upon the earth, wearing the shapes of men; and they married the fairest of the daughters of men. There were also giants on the earth in those days; and the sons of the fallen angels who married the daughters of men were stronger than any who have since lived.

As the years went by the hearts of most men and women were turned wholly to evil, and there was no room in them for kind or holy thoughts. Yet the evil did not come upon them all at once, and during the three hundred and fifty-three years when Enoch was king of the human race there was peace and justice in all lands.

But in the end Jahveh took Enoch to Heaven in a chariot of fire and his son Methuselah reigned after him. He too was a good king who followed in the way of righteousness as his father had taught him; but he could not turn the people from wickedness.

Yet one he trained to be one of the best of all men, and that was his grandson Noah. And after many years Jahveh chose Noah and his family out of all the people on earth to keep alive and carry on the human race when the wicked should be punished.

But first of all Jahveh sent down a Messenger—a faithful angel—to Methuselah and Noah, bearing his commands:

'Go and speak to all mankind and say: "These are the words of Jahveh, who created the world and all that is in it: turn from your evil desires, give up your wicked ways, and Jahveh will spare you and let you continue to live upon the earth. For Jahveh commands us to say that he gives you one hundred and twenty years in which to repent and mend your ways; but if you do not give up your evil ways, then he will bring destruction upon you all."'

So Noah and Methuselah went out and preached to the people each day from morning until night; but the people laughed at their warnings, and paid no attention to their words.

When the hundred and twenty years were drawing to a close, Noah married Naamah, the youngest daughter of Enoch. He was already five hundred years old—yet this was no more than middle age to the men of those days.

Noah had three sons called Shem, Ham and Japhet, and as soon as they were grown men they married and had families, in obedience to the will of Jahveh.

Then once again Jahveh sent his Messenger to Noah and Methuselah, saying: 'For the last time go out and call the people to repentance. If they turn from their evil ways, and from the worship of idols, Jahveh will spare them. But if not his punishment will fall upon all mankind.'

So the ancient king and his grandson went once more from city to city declaring the words of Jahveh to all peoples; but once again they were received with scorn, and men continued in their wicked ways and grew more evil day by day.

Not long after this Methuselah died, and then Jahveh spoke to Noah, saying: 'The end of my patience has come and the end of all living things is at hand. For the earth is filled with evil and violence, and I will destroy the earth, and all these wicked ones shall die.

'But you and yours shall live; for I do not propose to destroy life utterly, nor blot out the world and the living things in it which I have made. Therefore make an ark out of gopher wood, divided into rooms and covered both inside and outside with pitch to keep out the water. This ark shall be six hundred feet in length and a hundred feet wide and sixty feet high, with three decks like storeys one above the other. Make a door in its side, and two feet below the roof make a window.

'Build the Ark speedily, for I, Jahveh, who made the world, will destroy all living things that are not in the Ark. I will bring a flood of water over the earth to drown all things that breathe, and they shall all die. But you I will save; you shall go into the Ark, taking with you your wife and your sons and your sons' wives. And you shall take with you into the Ark a male and a female of all living creatures so that their kind may not perish from the earth: of all the birds of the air, of all the beasts of the field, and of everything that creeps on the ground—of every sort you must take two, and keep them alive. And store the Ark with food for all the creatures that you take into it; also take food for yourself and for your family—and do not let one creature that is in the Ark go short.'

Then Noah and his sons set to work and built the great Ark of refuge, while the people mocked at them.

But when it was complete, Jahveh once more spoke to Noah, saying: 'In seven days from now I will let loose rain over all the earth for forty days and forty nights until every living thing is drowned. So make haste to store the Ark with food, and on the sixth day the beasts of the earth and the birds of the sky will gather round. Stand in the doorway of the Ark and look forth: the creatures that lie down before you are those which come with you to safety. Let your sons lead them into the Ark, touching none of those that remain standing.'

Noah did as he was commanded, and by the seventh day all the creatures, two by two, had come aboard the Ark.

Then Noah preached once more to the people, warning them of what was about to happen. But when he found that not one of them would believe him, he went into the Ark with his wife and his sons and his sons' wives, and barred the door.

Next day the storm clouds gathered, the thunder roared, the lightning flashed, and the rain fell in such sheets that it seemed as if the very windows of the sky were opened.

For a little while Noah stood at the window of the Ark which was soon floating on the rising waters, gazing out at the drowning world.

A few of the people came and clung to the Ark, begging Noah to save them. But he shook his head sadly, for there was no room in the Ark for any more, and he said:

'For a hundred and twenty years I begged you to believe my words—now, alas, it is too late.'

Then Noah shut the window of the Ark and sealed it. The rain poured down harder and harder until Noah and his family cried out in terror; and all the animals in the Ark cried out also, each according to its kind, and the noise was so terrible that it almost crowned the roaring of the rain.

For forty days and forty nights the rain fell, and the Ark floated higher and higher. The great plains of Mesopotamia between the Tigris and Euphrates rivers were covered to the depth of nearly thirty feet, and nothing lived. All the creatures who walk upon the earth died—the cattle, the wild beasts, the creeping things, the birds, and every man, until all that breathed the air and made their homes upon dry land had perished.

Yet Noah and all those in the Ark were safe. After a hundred and fifty days the flood began to go down, and on the seventeenth day of the seventh month since the rain began, the Ark came to rest on the top of Mount Ararat. By the tenth month the tops of the hills were visible like islands in the sea, and Noah opened the window of the Ark and sent out a raven. But it flew to and fro, feeding on the corpses which still floated upon the waters.

So then Noah sent out a dove. But the dove found nowhere to rest, and it returned to the Ark and perched on Noah's hand. Seven days later he sent it out again, and in the evening it returned with a green olive leaf in its beak.

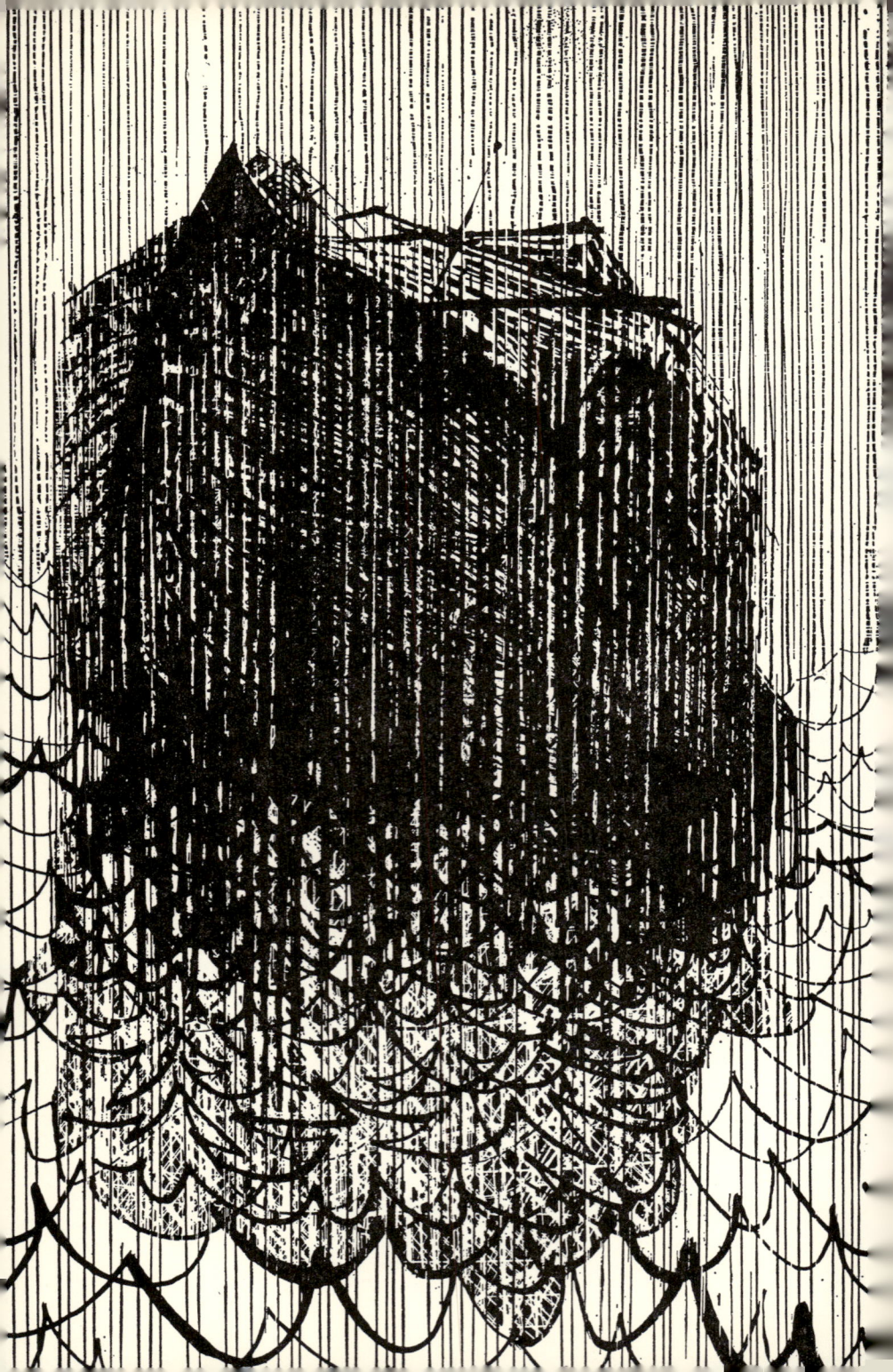

Then Noah knew that the waters had retreated far enough for the trees to be showing above them. And when, seven days later, he sent out the dove once more it did not come back.

Noah waited until the year had run its full course, and then he opened the door of the Ark and all the birds and beasts and creeping things went joyously forth and scattered over the earth.

Then Noah and his family came out also and knelt in prayer to Jahveh, thanking him for saving them from the Flood. And Jahveh spoke to Noah and his sons out of Heaven, saying:

'My blessing be upon you and yours. Be fruitful and multiply so that the earth may be peopled again. And tell to all mankind in the years to come that never again will I drown the earth in a great flood. See, I set my Bow in the clouds as a sign that the sun shall smile out speedily after the rain—and when your sons and their children to the end of time see the Rain Bow in the sky they shall rejoice, remembering my promise.

'But see to it that you and yours follow my law. Remember the fate of Cain and live in peace; for he who sheds man's blood, by man shall his blood be shed.'

And the blessing of Jahveh was upon Noah and his sons, and they became the ancestors of all mankind: Ham of the dark races of the southern lands, Shem of the nations of the east, and Japhet of the dwellers in the islands and of Europe.

. . . the rain fell, and the Ark floated higher and higher

THE TOWER OF BABEL

WHEN the earth was at last freed from the waters of the Flood, Noah and his children came down from the mountains onto the great plain of Mesopotamia which lies between the Tigris and Euphrates rivers.

Here, in the land which was then called Shinar, they settled and flourished greatly, until within three generations all the world was repeopled.

Now the world in those days, and to the grandchildren of Noah, was very little more than the land of Shinar, and all the people who dwelt in it still spoke the same language and were one nation.

Yet very soon they began to quarrel among themselves and, forgetting how the world had been destroyed in the Flood, to fall into all manner of wickedness almost as bad as in the days when Noah had preached in vain to the people.

Foremost among Noah's grandsons was Cush, the son of Ham. When he was already an old man he married a young wife, and they had a son called Nimrod—which means 'rebel', for already the people of Shinar were rebelling against the commands of Jahveh, and even beginning to worship other gods and make images and idols of them.

As Nimrod grew up his father loved him more and more—for he was the child of his old age, and it was natural for him to spoil him.

Now it chanced that when Adam was driven out of the Garden of Eden, Jahveh had given him a coat of skins to wear as protection against the thorns and briars of the outer world, and to give him strength to fight against all its dangers. This precious coat came to Enoch on Adam's death, and after him to Methusaleh, who gave it to Noah.

At the time of the Flood, Noah took it with him into the Ark as his most precious possession. Afterwards, when Noah had planted the first vineyard and become drunk on the first wine to be made in the world, his son Ham stole it and hid it away so that his brothers should not get it.

Before he died, however, Ham gave Adam's coat to Cush, and when Nimrod was twenty years old Cush gave it to him. Now there was still power in the coat, and as soon as he put it on, Nimrod was filled with strength. Very soon he became a mighty hunter in the fields and forests; and when Cush died and he became king he proved himself a mighty fighter also. So strong and reckless a fighter was he that very soon he became king of the whole world of Shinar.

His last great battle was against his cousins, the sons of Japhet, who until then had been the most powerful in the land.

But Nimrod gathered his army together and said:

'Children of Ham, my people, do not be afraid. Banish all fear from your hearts and follow me. I promise you that we shall be victorious; our enemies shall become your slaves, and you can do with them as you please.'

Then Nimrod's followers cheered loudly, and rushed into battle behind him. They defeated their enemies and made the descendants of Japhet their servants. And after this they crowned Nimrod as King of the World.

When he had come to power, Nimrod chose the site for his great capital city on the banks of the Euphrates—the city that was afterwards called Babylon. As it grew he gathered wealth into it, with slaves and women, until in his pride he began to equal himself with Jahveh.

Indeed Nimrod paid little reverence to Jahveh, making costly images of other gods, and encouraging his people and his son Prince Mordon to worship idols.

Presently the great lords of Nimrod's court, and the princes of the blood royal, grew prouder still. And they said among themselves:

Higher still grew the tower

'Let us build a mighty tower, higher than any tower in the world. Let us make it so high that it reaches right into Heaven! Then men and gods will tremble and bow down before us, and know that we are greater than any of them.'

When Nimrod heard of this scheme he was filled with delight, and his own pride grew higher still.

So they chose a place not far from the city of Babylon; and the people turned out in thousands to join in the building of the tower. They made bricks of mud and straw, and baked them hard. And they made a base hundreds of yards square, and began to build the tower, mortaring the bricks together course by course with the thick black bitumen of which there were several lakes in Shinar.

As the tower rose higher and higher, so the pride and boastfulness of Nimrod and his people grew with it.

'We will build our tower right up to Heaven,' they said; 'then we will put the statues of our gods there, and go up into Heaven to worship them.'

The tower grew higher still, and they said:

'We will march an army up the tower and into Heaven and frighten Jahveh into obeying us.'

THE TOWER OF BABEL

Higher still grew the tower, and Nimrod and his builders cried:
'If Jahveh will not obey us, we'll fight him and conquer him with our arrows and spears, and make him our slave. What can Jahveh do against so great a king as Nimrod, or against people who have conquered the whole world and built so mighty a tower?'

So they worked on—and if a block of stone or a mass of masonry chanced to fall, they wept and lamented. But if one of the slaves who were forced to labour at the building as it neared the clouds fell to his death, they only laughed.

Then at last Jahveh showed his anger and punished the pride of Nimrod and his lords. Suddenly a confusion of tongues fell upon them, and for the first time each spoke a different language, and could not understand one another's speech.

They shouted their commands in vain; and when they were not obeyed—because they could not be understood—they began fighting among themselves. And so the building of the tower came to an end, and the builders with their followers and children separated angrily and moved away to settle in different parts of the earth.

As for the great, useless tower of Babel, Jahveh struck it with his lightning so that a third of it fell to the ground. A third of it sank into the earth; but one-third stands even to this day, a towering ruin—and in the evening the shadow of that hideous strength lies across the desert for many thousands of feet, and yet comes no nearer to Heaven than the tower did.

Book Two

THE FAMILY OF ISRAEL

THE ADVENTURES OF ABRAHAM

ALTHOUGH the tower of Babel had been struck by Jahveh, and many of its builders had moved away to found cities of their own with those who now spoke the same languages, King Nimrod still ruled in Babylon.

Not long after the 'confusion of tongues' at Babel, the wife of Nimrod's chief officer and favourite cousin Therach bore a son called Abraham. To celebrate this event Therach held a great feast to which he invited many of the wise men and magicians from King Nimrod's court.

As they came out into the night, an hour before the dawning, the wise men and magicians saw a strange sight in the dark sky. A bright star moved across the darkness out of the east, and as it passed it seemed to swallow up or consume four other stars which until then had hung low in the sky over the great city of Babylon.

'This is surely a sign, an omen of the future,' said the magicians among themselves. 'It tells of this child Abraham, the son of Therach. When he grows up he will become the father of a great nation that in time to come will destroy this kingdom and possess its lands.'

Next day, when they discussed the wonder they had seen, the magicians said to one another: 'It would be best if we told King Nimrod concerning the omen of the star of Abraham. For if he learns of it from others his anger will be great against us, and he may even cause us to be slain.'

So the magicians sought audience with the king, and when they were come into his presence the leader of them bowed low and said:

'O King, live for ever, we have seen a wonder and by our wisdom we have learned of its meaning.'

And when the magician had told all his tale to Nimrod he ended: 'O King, live for ever, our advice to you is that you pay Therach the price of this child and destroy it while it is yet an infant—lest in days to come we and our children should be utterly destroyed by him and his descendants.'

Nimrod listened to all that the magicians had to say, and when they had finished he rewarded them and sent them away.

But as soon as they were gone he bade a messenger command Therach's instant presence. And when he stood before him Nimrod said:

'My friend and cousin, listen to what has been revealed to my magicians.' And when he had repeated all their words he ended: 'Therefore, true and faithful friend, give me the child so that he may be slain before misfortune comes upon us, and I will give you thrice his weight in gold, and fill your coffers with silver.'

Then Therach answered: 'O King, live for ever, I have listened to your words and as always I am your humble and obedient servant. Yet first let me seek of your great wisdom by telling you of a request that was made to me yesterday and asking you to advise me on my answer.'

'It is well,' said Nimrod; 'ask on.'

'Yesterday', answered Therach, 'Ayon, the son of Morad,

came to my house desiring to purchase the beautiful steed which you, O King, gave me not long ago. "Sell the horse to me," said Ayon, "and besides its full value I will fill your stables with straw and provender." But I answered him that I could not part with the king's gift without the king's permission; and now, O King, live for ever, I ask your advice.'

Then Nimrod sprang up in a rage, crying: 'How can you dare to think of parting with the steed I gave to you, the finest in all the land, for mere gold and straw and provender? Surely you are not so poor that you stand in need of any of these things?'

Therach bowed before Nimrod and made answer, 'O King, live for ever, I thank you for your words, and I will obey them. Moreover, if you feel thus about the horse, how can you ask me to part with my child? Gold and silver cannot pay me for the gift which my king made to me; silver and gold cannot pay for the child which Jahveh has given me.'

Nimrod said nothing, but he glared at Therach with such fury that he made haste to add:

'All my possessions are but held in trust. They are my king's, yes, even my child, and he may take them without money and without price.'

'Not so!' exclaimed Nimrod, 'I will buy the child, and fill your coffers with gold and silver.'

'Then, my lord,' said Therach, 'give me three days in which to see how I may break this matter to my wife, the boy's mother.'

Nimrod granted this request. But at the end of three days he sent a message bidding Therach bring the child forthwith, or he and all his family should be put to death.

Then Therach took the child of one of his slaves, a baby boy who had been born on the same day as Abraham, and carried him to Nimrod, who caused it to be slain forthwith and gave him coffers of gold and silver in exchange.

But Therach hid his wife and the baby Abraham in a cave hard by the city of Ur of the Chaldees, sending them food secretly every week. And Abraham dwelt in this cave until he was ten years old.

By this time Nimrod and his counsellors had forgotten all about him, and he was able to dwell quietly in Ur of the Chaldees with Noah—who lived for three hundred and fifty years after the Flood, as well as six hundred years before it.

For thirty-nine years Abraham lived with Noah, learning all the wisdom of the days before the Flood, and of how Jahveh had punished the wicked and saved only those who worshipped him truly.

When he was fifty Abraham paid his first visit to Babylon, and found that even his own father Therach had forgotten Jahveh and had made twelve images of wood which he worshipped as gods.

Horrified at the sight of these images, Abraham waited until his father was out of the house, and then took an axe and destroyed eleven of them.

Scarcely had he done this when Therach returned. He was filled with wrath and horror at the sight, and cried out:

'What wickedness have you done to my gods?'

'I brought them food as I had seen you do,' answered Abraham, 'and the god who still stands here seized an axe and destroyed the other eleven so that he could have all the food to himself.'

'This is a wicked lie!' shouted Therach. 'I made these gods with my own hands out of wood. They can neither eat nor destroy each other with any implement!'

'Then why worship senseless, powerless lumps of wood?" asked Abraham. 'There is only one true God, who made heaven and earth and all things in them—and saved our forbear Noah with all his family in the Ark when the great Flood came to destroy those who worshipped such idols as these. Cease from calling the work of your hands gods, and worship Jahveh before some terrible punishment come upon you. See, this god of yours can neither defend himself nor be revenged upon his destroyer!'

So saying Abraham seized the axe and chopped up the last reamining idol into fragments, which he cast onto the fire.

When Therach saw what his son did he turned without a word

and hastened into the presence of King Nimrod. Falling on the ground before him he cried:

'O King, live for ever, a son of mine, born fifty years ago, has destroyed the twelve gods who stood in my house, and spoken insulting words of them. Therefore I beg you have him brought before you and judged according to the laws of Babylon.'

When Abraham stood before the king Nimrod said: 'Son of Therach, what is this evil which you have done to your father's gods?'

Then Abraham told the same story which he had spoken to his father and, like Therach, Nimrod exclaimed:

'These are but vain and lying words! The gods of wood and stone whom we worship in Babylon have no power to do such things.'

'Then why do you serve them?' asked Abraham. 'Why let your subjects practise such folly and wickedness? Teach them rather to serve Jahveh who alone has power to kill or to keep alive.'

When Nimrod and his court heard these words they cried out in fury. And presently the king uttered his command:

'Guard Abraham in prison until the third day from now. And build a fiery furnace in the great square of Babylon where all may see. When the fiery furnace is heated cast him into it—and see if his god can save him then, and has power of life and death!'

Now when the magicians saw Abraham they knew by their arts that he was the child at whose birth the great star had devoured the smaller stars. When they told this to the king, Nimrod was minded to fling Therach into the fiercy furnace with Abraham. But Therach cried out in a mad panic:

'O King, live for ever, it was not at my command that Abraham was saved, but by the guile of my elder son Charan!'

'Then let Charan be cast into the fiercy furnace with Abraham!' commanded Nimrod, and nothing that Therach could say served to make him change his mind.

Charan, as a matter of fact, was a man without faith or purpose.

After Abraham had destroyed the idols he said: 'I shall wait and see which gods are the most powerful: if Abraham is saved I'll worship Jahveh. If not, the gods of Babylon.'

He was still undecided when the third day dawned and the great furnace in the main square of Babylon was heated until no one could go near it. But Abraham said simply:

'Jahveh will preserve me, if it his will to show this wicked king that there is no other God save he who created the world and set our ancestor Adam in the Garden of Eden.'

With all the people of Babylon gathered to see the show, Abraham and Charan were brought out of the prison and led before Nimrod. Abraham remained proudly silent, while Charan cried aloud for mercy, assuring the king that he was a true worshipper of the gods of Babylon and did not even know that Abraham was his brother.

In spite of this, however, both were stripped of their robes, their hands and feet were bound together, and they were cast into the burning fiery furnace.

Now the heat of that furnace was so great that twelve of Nimrod's men who cast them into it were burned to death while doing so. As for Charan, he was consumed to ashes before ever he reached the bottom of the furnace.

But Jahveh willed otherwise with Abraham, and presently the king's servants, peeping into the furnace, started back in fear and amazement, crying:

'Look! Abraham is walking about unharmed in the midst of the flames! The ropes which bound him are burned to ashes, but he is not even scorched!'

At first Nimrod would not believe them. 'Bring him out then if he is unharmed!' he commanded. 'Make haste, in case he dies!'

But it was the king's servants who died, for when they drew near the furnace the flames blazed out in their faces and consumed many of them.

Then Nimrod became frightened, and called aloud: 'Abraham, servant of Jahveh the true God, come out of the fire and stand before me!'

And Abraham stepped quietly out of the furnace and stood before Nimrod, with not so much as one lock of hair on his head singed by the heat.

Then Nimrod and his courtiers would have worshipped Abraham as a god; but he cried:

'Do not bow down to me, for I am only a man even as you are. Bow down rather to Jahveh who made you, and who has preserved me from the flames.'

After this Nimrod loaded Abraham with riches and sent him with all honour back to Ur of the Chaldees, bidding him rule it as his governor.

Nevertheless, after a little while Nimrod decided to send an army to slay Abraham, for he had further dreams which his magicians told him meant that Abraham's descendants would indeed conquer Babylon and all the land of Shinar.

This time Jahveh spoke to Abraham, telling him in his heart that he and all his family and followers should set out from Ur of the Chaldees and seek a new home for themselves in the land of Canaan far away to the north-west where the same sea beat on the coast that washed the lands where Japhet's descendants dwelt.

So Abraham set out from Ur with his wife Sarah and his nephew Lot, their families, their flocks and their herds. And after a long trek they came safely into the land of Canaan—which in after days was called Palestine—and settled on the hills of Bethel above the Jordan valley.

Here they dwelt for some years, leaving the land only once during a famine when they crossed the desert into Egypt where there was much corn.

When they returned to Canaan their flocks and herds had increased so greatly that there was no longer room for them all on the hills of Bethel. So Lot and his family went down into the valley of the Jordan to dwell with the Canaanites in and about Sodom and the other cities of the plain.

Now it chanced that the people who lived in these cities were as wicked as any in Babylon or any whom Jahveh had drowned in the great Flood. In their daily life they were cruel and treacherous, stealing from innocent traders who came to their land and beating or killing them. Moreover they mocked at Jahveh and did not worship him or obey his laws; instead, they had planted a great garden in the valley where they gathered frequently to worship idols and perform horrible and sinful rites in their honour.

At home in their cities they were every bit as vile; and no man, woman or child was safe in the streets after nightfall.

Seeing the wickedness of the Cities of the Plain, Jahveh sent three of his Messengers down to the land of Canaan.

They appeared as three handsome young men; and first of all they visited Abraham in his camp near Bethel.

Abraham sat at the door of his tent, and when he saw the three strangers he hastened to welcome them with bread and wine, and knelt down to wash their feet.

Presently the three visitors told Abraham that they were the Messengers of Jahveh, and one of them said to him:

'Abraham, call hither your wife Sarah, for we have a message for her.'

Sarah was in the tent, cooking veal for the guests, and she came out when Abraham bade her.

'Sarah,' said one of the Messengers, 'the time is drawing near when you shall bear a son to be your joy and the delight of Abraham your husband.'

But Sarah laughed, saying: 'Surely, sir, you do but jest. We are old, my husband and I—and I am far past the age at which it is possible for a woman to bear a child.'

For a moment the Messenger seemed to shine with light and his voice echoed like distant thunder as he cried:

'Do you doubt the word of Jahveh? Nothing is impossible to the maker of all things!'

Sarah fled back into the tent, denying in her fear that she had laughed.

But the Messengers smiled, and rising from their seats they beckoned Abraham to follow them to the edge of the hill.

There they paused and looked down into the rich valley of the Jordan with the Dead Sea lying deep and blue in the distance and the mountains of Moab growing pink beyond it in the evening light.

The Cities of the Plain lay in the richly fertile land on either side of where the river flowed into the sea, and Sodom, the greatest of them, was clearly visible.

'We are sent also to the Cities of the Plain,' said the Messengers. 'Because of their wickedness Jahveh will destroy them with fire and brimstone.'

'Surely Jahveh will not let the good perish with the evil!' cried Abraham. 'Perhaps there are fifty virtuous men in each of the cities: will not Jahveh spare the place for their sake?'

'They shall be warned,' answered the Messenger. 'If they turn from their wickedness they shall live. We go now to Sodom, and there first of all will visit your nephew Lot.'

As dusk was beginning to fall two of Jahveh's Messengers, in the likeness of handsome young men, were knocking at Lot's door in Sodom.

Lot and his wife welcomed them in and set a fine dinner before them, waiting on them as if they were great lords—though as yet they did not know who or what they were.

But they had not reached Lot's house unseen. Later that evening a band of the wicked young Sodomites came and surrounded the house, beating on the doors and shouting:

'Where are the beautiful young men who came to visit you? Bring them out and give them to us!'

Then Lot went out into the street, shutting the door behind him, and trying to reason with the Sodomites, saying:

'Brothers, what you intend to do is so wicked that Jahveh will surely bring destruction upon you and all in this city. Remember moreover that these men are guests, and so are sacred.'

The Sodomites shouted and jeered, and made as if to push him aside, and Lot cried:

'Spare these two men, my guests, and I will let you have my two daughters; for this at least will be a lesser sin.'

But the Sodomites shouted: 'Stand back! Do not dare to make yourself our judge—you who are only a stranger!'

Then it would have gone hard with Lot had not the two Messengers suddenly appeared in the doorway behind him.

At once all the Sodomites who looked at them seemed to be dazzled as by a flash of lightning or a sudden beam of the midday sun. The Messengers drew Lot into the house and shut the door; and it seemed to all the Sodomites outside that they could see nothing but darkness. In vain they groped to find the door, and at last wandered blindly away into the dark city.

But inside the house the Messengers were telling Lot why they had come, and they said to him:

'If you know of any of the people of Sodom who are worthy to be saved, or if you have sons and daughters living in the city, go at once and bid them flee up to the hills before day dawns. For Jahveh will destroy all the Cities of the Plain because of such wickedness as you strove to save us from tonight.'

So Lot went in haste to his sons-in-law who had married his other daughters, and to their kinsmen, warning them of the wrath to come. But they laughed at him, and told him not to disturb them again with such foolish words.

Lot returned sadly home, and the Messengers said:

'Make haste now. Take your wife and your two unmarried daughters and flee up into the hills. We will lead you out of the city, and you will be able to find your way across the plain and up to the hills, the tops of which will be shining in the light of the rising sun. But do not any of you look behind until you are in the full daylight on the hillside of Zoar.'

Swiftly the Messengers led Lot and his family out of Sodom. And Lot lifted up his eyes to the hills and saw the light of the rising sun striking upon the rocky cliffs like a beacon. Then, with his eyes fixed upon the light, he hastened across the plain and up the steep slope beyond.

. . . he could see the flare of burning Sodom

Behind him he heard sounds of terror and of dread, and with the tail of his eye could see the flare of burning Sodom.

'Forward!' he cried. 'Remember the commands of Jahveh's Messengers!'

But as they reached the beginning of the slope Lot's wife could no longer restrain her curiosity and her anxiety for those whom she had left behind. She turned and looked back towards Sodom—and on that instant was turned into a pillar of salt.

Lot and his daughters, however, came out into the bright sunshine high on the mountain, and turned in safety to look back into the valley of Jordan.

There flowed the river, and the Dead Sea was already blue once more. But from the plain on either side of Jordan the smoke went up from the places where the cities had stood which Jahveh had destroyed that night with fire and brimstone.

And that plain is a desert of salt and rock to this day.

ISAAC AND REBEKAH

Jahveh did not forget his promise to Sarah made by the Messengers. For when she was ninety years of age she bore a son to Abraham, who was a hundred, and they called the child Isaac.

When Isaac was a year old Abraham held a great feast in his honour and in honour of Sarah, and there was much rejoicing.

And Sarah said: 'Jahveh has sent me happiness. I laugh with joy, and all who hear me laugh with me. For I have borne Abraham a son to comfort him in his old age.'

But she was jealous, and drove out Abraham's other son, Ishmael, whom a slave-girl called Hagar had borne to him in Egypt. However, Jahveh sent a Messenger to protect Hagar and her son, and to tell her that Ishmael too should be the father of a great nation—of those wandering nomads who dwelt in tents and afterwards became the great Arab race.

Meanwhile Isaac grew into a strong and handsome boy, the idol of his parents and the light of their eyes.

But it seemed as if Jahveh grew jealous of all the love lavished upon Isaac. For one day he sent a Messenger to Abraham as he sat alone on the hillside.

And the Messenger said: 'Abraham, I am sent from heaven by Jahveh himself with his commands to you. And thus says Jahveh: "Take your son, your only son Isaac, whom you love above all things, and go with him into the land of Moriah up among the western mountains, to the rocky hill top which my Messenger will show you, and there offer Isaac to me as a burnt sacrifice."'

Abraham grieved sorely when he heard this. But he answered the Messenger quietly: 'Whatever Jahveh commands, that will I do.'

When the Messenger had vanished Abraham went slowly home. He said nothing to Sarah about Jahveh's command, but he told her that next day he and Isaac were going up into the mountains to offer sacrifice.

'Our son will soon no longer be a child,' he said, 'and he has not yet learned the service of heaven.'

'Go, my lord,' answered Sarah, 'but do not take the lad any great distance, for he is still young—and I cannot bear him out of my sight for long.'

And Abraham said: 'While we are gone, pray for the happiness of our son, and for my happiness, and for your own.'

Next morning Abraham rose up early and saddled his ass, and took two serving men with him and Isaac his son, and set out as Jahveh had commanded. The ass was loaded with faggots of dry wood for the burnt offering, since the mountain might be one on which no trees grew.

They went up from the valley of the Jordan by easy stages among the mountains, and on the third day came to a valley with a long rocky hill in the midst of it—the place where Jerusalem, the Holy City, would be built in after days.

When they came in sight of it, Jahveh put it into Abraham's heart that this was the place of sacrifice. So he said to the serving men: 'Stay here and look after the ass, and the lad and I will go up onto the hill over there to worship and return later.'

Then Abraham took the faggots for the burnt offering and fastened them upon Isaac's shoulders. And he himself took the fire-pot of burning charcoal they had brought with them, and made sure that the sacrificial knife was in his belt.

As they went up the hillside Isaac said: 'My father, the wood for the burnt offering is on my back, and you carry the fire and the knife; but where is the lamb we are to sacrifice?'

Abraham answered: 'My son, Jahveh will provide a lamb for the burnt offering, never fear.'

So they went on until they came to the rocky hill top where in after years the temple was to stand, and later still the Dome of the Rock. And here Abraham built an altar and placed the wood upon it, and then said to Isaac:

'My son, Jahveh has chosen you, a creature without blemish, to be a burnt offering to his glory in place of a lamb. He sent a Messenger from heaven to tell me this, and now I must sacrifice you, though it break my heart and your mother's heart. For the command of God comes before the will of man.'

Then Isaac answered bravely: 'If Jahveh bids it I will obey in thankfulness.'

Abraham then asked: 'Tell me, my son, keeping nothing back in this great hour, is there any secret evil in your heart, or any wrong upon your mind?'

Isaac thought for a little, and then he said: 'I swear before Jahveh that I know of no evil and regret nothing. Blessed be the great God who has desired me this day.'

So Abraham placed Isaac upon the altar, and Isaac spoke again, saying:

'Father, bind me tightly lest against my will I may struggle and so spoil the sacrifice. And when my body is burnt in the fire, take my ashes to my mother and tell her that they are all that remain of her son Isaac whom Jahveh gave and has now taken away.'

When Abraham heard these words he wept bitterly, but Isaac said, 'Quickly now, Father: do the will of Jahveh,' and he stretched his neck to receive the knife which Abraham held ready in his hand.

But as Abraham raised the knife to perform the sacrifice a voice cried suddenly:

'Abraham! Abraham! Do not slay your son! Jahveh has seen how truly you worship him—so truly that you would not even deny him the life of your beloved son. He has sent me, his Messenger, to bid you release Isaac so that he may help you to perform the sacrifice for which the victim is waiting over there behind you.'

Abraham turned and saw a ram caught in a thicket by its horns. So he untied Isaac, and the two of them took the ram and bound it upon the altar and sacrificed it to Jahveh.

When it was consumed the Messenger spoke again, saying:

'Abraham, because of your obedience Jahveh has decreed that your descendants shall multiply and increase like the stars of heaven. They shall be the Chosen People who know that there is but one God and worship him alone. In time to come this shall be their land, and they shall dwell in it for as long as they prove worthy, and from them shall come a blessing in which the whole world shall have part.'

Abraham and Isaac knelt in prayer; and when they looked up the Messenger had vanished into heaven.

So they went down the hill in silent happiness to where the serving men waited. And they set out for home with Isaac riding on the ass.

But while Abraham and Isaac were on their way an old man came to Sarah's tent and said to her:

'It has been revealed to me that Abraham has offered up Isaac as a sacrifice to Jahveh. Yes, in spite of his struggles and his cries, your son has been slain with the knife and consumed with fire.'

Then Sarah uttered a heart-rending cry, and throwing herself on the ground wept and lamented.

When she looked up the old man had gone. So she called her servants and set out to look for Abraham. Not finding him, she returned sadly to her tent and there was met by the same old man, who greeted her, saying:

'Although Abraham set out to slay his son in sacrifice, Jahveh has spared him. See where they come over the hillside yonder.'

When Sarah looked up and saw that her beloved son was indeed alive and safe, the shock was too much for her. Grief she had been able to survive, but her joy was so great that she sank down and died of sheer happiness.

Abraham and Isaac mourned for long over Sarah's death; and indeed Isaac's grief was so great that nothing seemed able to bring him comfort.

At last Abraham decided to take the matter into his own hands. So he sent for his steward—the senior servant in his house—whose name was Eliezer, and said to him:

'The time has come to find a wife for my son Isaac. I grow old, and I desire to see him married, and to bless my grandchildren before I die. Therefore swear to me by the most solemn of oaths that you will do all that I bid you; and then I will send you forth to the land from which I came to find a wife for Isaac. For you shall swear that you will indeed go to Ur of the Chaldees and bring him as wife the daughter of one of my own people and not of the Canaanites among whom I dwell.'

Then Eliezer said: 'My lord, I will do all that you bid me. But supposing that the maiden of Ur will not come with me? Should I not take Isaac your son as my companion so that he can woo and win her?'

But Abraham answered: 'Isaac shall not go to Ur of the Chaldees, and you must swear never to lead or accompany him thither. Here he must bide, for Jahveh has promised that my descendants shall rule all this land. Moreover he will send his Messenger to Ur of the Chaldees, or bring it to pass in some way that you will choose the right maiden and she will come willingly.'

So Eliezer swore the oath to Abraham. Then he set off, taking ten of his master's camels laden with presents and stores and other goods; and he crossed the mountains and the deserts until he came to Mesopotamia, to Ur of the Chaldees.

He arrived in the evening and made his camels kneel down outside the city by a well of water; for he knew that it was near the hour when the women of Ur would come out with their pitchers to draw water.

And Eliezer prayed to Jahveh, saying: 'O God of my master Abraham, send me good speed this day and show kindness to your servant. I stand here by the well, and the daughters of the men of this city will soon be coming to draw water. May it happen that the maiden to whom I shall say, "Let down your pitcher, I beg you, so that I may drink", shall reply, "Drink, and

I will bring water to your camels also"—may she be the bride whom you have appointed for Isaac, my master's son.'

Scarcely had Eliezer finished speaking when the maidens of Ur came out carrying their empty pitchers on their shoulders. As the first and fairest approached him, Eliezer bowed down before her and said:

'Maiden, I beg you to let me drink from your pitcher, for I am parched after journeying across the desert.'

And she answered: 'Drink, and I will bring water to your camels also.'

As soon as she had filled the troughs, and the camels were drinking, Eliezer took golden earrings and two golden bracelets out of his pack and offered them to her, saying:

'Tell me, I beg of you, whose daughter are you? And furthermore is there room in your father's house for us to lodge?'

She answered at once: 'My name is Rebekah, and I am the daughter of Bethuel, the son of Milcah and Nahor.'

'Now praise be to Jahveh!' exclaimed Eliezer. 'I am the servant of Abraham, the brother of your grandfather Nahor—and Jahveh has led me straight to my master's family.'

Then Rebekah took the golden ornaments and hastened into the city, where she told her father and her brother Laban all that had happened.

At once Laban set off for the well and led Eliezer and his camels into the city, to Bethuel's house, saying: 'Come with me, you whom Jahveh has blessed: our house awaits you, and there are stables for your camels.'

So Eliezer followed Laban into Ur, and was welcomed by Bethuel and his family. Before he would touch food he told them his story: of how Abraham had prospered in the land of the Canaanites, and had sent him to bring a wife for his son Isaac, from among his relatives at Ur, and of how Jahveh had guided him so that the first person he spoke to was Rebekah.

Then Bethuel and Laban said: 'This is indeed Jahveh's doing. There is no more for us to say. If Rebekah is willing, then she shall set out immediately to be Isaac's wife and the mother of the great race to whom Jahveh has promised the land of Canaan.'

'I am willing,' said Rebekah. 'Tomorrow let us set out. For we must not tarry in obeying Jahveh's commands.'

Next day, accordingly, Eliezer led Rebekah and her servants out of Ur. They crossed the desert by easy stages, and came through the mountains to where the tents of Abraham were pitched on the hillside looking down into the valley of the Jordan.

That evening Isaac had gone out alone into the fields to meditate. As he walked he lifted up his eyes and saw Eliezer's caravan approaching. On the foremost camel sat the most beautiful maiden he had ever seen.

As he stood lost in amazement Eliezer exclaimed: 'See! There is my master, Isaac!'

Rebekah looked for a moment, and then made haste to fasten her veil. But in the moment when their eyes had met Isaac and Rebekah loved each other. And next day they were married, and Isaac found all the joy of life return to him and was comforted for his mother's death.

ESAU AND JACOB

Isaac was truly happy in his marriage with Rebekah, and she was able to bring him comfort some years later when Abraham died at the age of a hundred and seventy-five.

But for a long time they had no children, and it was only after nineteen years that she bore Isaac twins, whose names were Esau and Jacob.

Now, although they were twins, Esau came into the world a moment before Jacob, and so he counted as the elder son. As they grew up Esau became a cunning hunter and a man of outdoor life, while Jacob was a tent-dweller and a shepherd.

Of the two Isaac loved Esau best because he was for ever bringing him spoils of the chase: tasty game as a change from mutton. But Rebekah loved Jacob, and tried always to put him first.

Now Esau hunted far away across the mountains and the deserts, and on his expeditions he sometimes met that other great hunter Nimrod, the aged king of Babylon.

Esau was a man of quick passions and violent thoughts, and he grew to be madly jealous of Nimrod and to hate him. And one day as he hunted in the mountains on the edge of the desert he saw Nimrod galloping across the sand towards him with only two followers, having left the rest of his hunters far behind.

At once Esau's jealousy and hate got the better of him. Slipping from his horse, he hid behind a rock, and as Nimrod passed he bent his bow and released an arrow which passed through his heart. Then, drawing his sword, Esau attacked Nimrod's two followers, and after a furious battle killed them both.

In haste he stripped from Nimrod's shoulder the wonderful

coat of skins which had belonged to Adam, and mounting his horse rode off in furious haste up into the mountains away from where the whole cavalcade of Babylonian hunters was already gathering round their murdered master.

All night and all the next day Esau rode through the mountains, and at last on the following evening, almost fainting with hunger and weariness, he came to his brother's tent.

Now Jacob had just made himself a rich and savoury meal of red lentils which was steaming in the pot as Esau staggered up to the tent.

'Feed me!' gasped Esau. 'Give me some of your red pottage, for I am fainting with hunger and tiredness.'

Jacob saw his chance, and said gently, as he stirred the lentils so that the evening breeze carried the steam to Esau's nostrils:

'Sell to me your birthright. Let me take all that is due to the first-born. *Then* I will give you as much of the red pottage as you desire.'

'I am at the point of death!' gasped Esau. 'And if I do not die of hunger tonight, doubtless King Nimrod's warriors will find me out and slay me tomorrow. Yes, I vow before Jahveh that you shall have my place as elder son and all that belongs to it. Give me in exchange food so that I do not fall dead here and now.'

So Jacob let Esau help himself to as much food as he wished. But he kept him to his bargain, in spite of the fact that no warriors came seeking Esau to avenge the death of Nimrod, who was carried back to burial in Babylon. But his death at Esau's hand was the first fulfilment of the prophecy that the Star of Abraham should blot out the star of Nimrod, and that Abraham's children and descendants would be a greater nation than Babylon itself.

But after he had sold him his birthright for a mess of pottage Esau hated Jacob his brother more than ever. Yet so long as Isaac lived he dared not try to murder him.

However, in time Isaac grew feeble and blind, and his sons saw that he had not long to live. Then Rebekah sought more and more eagerly for some way in which she could win even greater fortune for her favourite son; and Jacob thought day and night of how he could cheat his father and his brother so that he might become even more powerful and wealthy.

At last the chance came one morning when Isaac called for Esau and said:

'My son, take your bow in your hand and shoot for me a young deer. Then make for me a tender stew of the meat which I love—and when you bring it to me I will give you my blessing and make you the heir to the promise that Jahveh made to my father Abraham and to me—and your descendants shall rule over all this land, and through them shall come the greatest blessing of all to the whole world.'

Esau kissed his father, took his bow and quiver of arrows, and set out into a nearby valley among the mountains in quest of deer.

But Rebekah had heard all that Isaac said, and at once she drew Jacob aside and told him, ending:

'Obey all that I tell you, and you shall steal the blessing which Isaac intends for Esau his favourite. First of all, go swiftly to your flocks and kill two young kids; skin them and bring them to me, and I will make a savoury stew such as your father loves. Then he will eat it and bless you before he dies.'

Jacob answered, however: 'My father will know that it is I and not my brother who brings him the meat and asks his blessing. For Esau is a hairy man and I am a smooth man—and my father, being blind, will feel me to see that it is indeed Esau and find that instead it is Jacob, and he will lay no blessing upon me, but some terrible curse.'

'Let any curse rest on me,' answered Rebekah. 'Do as I tell you, and I will show you how to cheat your father still further.'

So Jacob went among his goats, killed two kids, and brought them to his mother. And Rebekah made just such a savoury stew as Isaac delighted in. And when it was ready she cut out pieces of the skins of the kids and put them over Jacob's hands and round his neck with the hairy side outwards.

Then Jacob made haste to carry the food into Isaac's tent, and he knelt before him, saying:

'My father, here am I, your son, who has brought you the food even as you commanded. Therefore, I pray you, take the food and give me your blessing.'

But Isaac, although his mouth watered at the smell of the savoury stew, feared some trick and said:

'Who are you?'

'Your son Esau,' answered Jacob.

'And how have you managed to slay a deer and bring me the venison so quickly?'

'Because Jahveh brought it to me as soon as I reached the valley,' replied Jacob.

Still doubting, Isaac said: 'Come near so that I may feel you and know even in my darkness that you are indeed my beloved son Esau whom I love above all things.'

Jacob went near, and Isaac felt the back of his hands and his neck, and said:

'Though your voice sounds more like the smooth voice of Jacob, your hands are the hands of Esau. Yet swear to me that you are indeed he.'

'I am surely Esau,' answered Jacob, setting the stew in his father's hands, and waiting on him while he ate and drank.

When he had finished Isaac said: 'Come nearer still, Esau my beloved, and kiss me.'

Jacob drew near and betrayed his brother with a kiss; and, being still deceived, Isaac called down a blessing on him, saying:

'May Jahveh give you the wealth of the earth and of corn and wine. Let the people serve you and the nations bow down to you, and let all members of my family obey you, and may my curse rest on any who would work you evil, and my blessing on all that wish you well.'

Jacob had scarcely received Isaac's blessing and left his presence when Esau returned from hunting.

Very soon he was kneeling before Isaac with a savoury stew in his hands and saying:

'Let my father accept this venison which I his son have for him so that he may take delight in it and cause his blessing to rest upon me.'

'Who are you?' asked Isaac in surprise.

'I am Esau, your first-born son,' was the answer.

Then Isaac began to shake and tremble, and he cried: 'Who do you say you are? Where is he who brought me a savoury stew of venison a little while ago before you came, saying that he was Esau my first-born? For I have given him my blessing, and what I have done I cannot now undo: he shall be blessed.'

When Esau heard this he cried aloud in his grief, and said: 'Father, bless me—give me your blessing too!'

But Isaac said: 'Now I perceive that your brother has deceived me and taken your blessing.'

'He is rightly named Jacob!' cried Esau in bitter anger—for 'Jacob' means 'a supplanter'. 'Twice over has he supplanted me: first he took my birthright, and now he has stolen my blessing. But, Father, have you no blessing reserved for me?'

'I have made him your lord and master,' said Isaac sadly, 'and all his kin I have given to him for servants. I have blessed him with corn and wine and the wealth of the earth—there is but little left for you. Yet you too shall prosper; you shall live by the sword, and serve your brother—and in the end you shall break away from him and found a nation in Edom over yonder beyond the Dead Sea.'

Esau went back to his own tents, breathing threats of vengeance against Jacob, and saying to his followers: 'My father cannot live long. As soon as he is buried, and we have done mourning for him, I will slay my brother Jacob and take back all that he has stolen from me.'

These words were reported to Rebekah, and she warned Jacob to be careful, and made with him a plan for his safety and advancement.

She was easily able to get round Isaac and make him think that the plan was his own; and in the end he sent for Jacob and said:

'My son, it is not right that you should marry a daughter of the Canaanites any more than I did. So now I bid you set out alone to Ur of the Chaldees. Go to the home of Bethuel, your mother's father, and choose a wife from among your cousins, the daughters of your uncle Laban. And now, lest I be no longer living when you return, I repeat my blessing on you. May the blessing that Jahveh promised to Abraham be upon you; may you rule all this land which was promised to Abraham, and be the father of a great people.'

So Jacob bade farewell to Isaac and Rebekah, and with his staff in his hand set out to the north into the mountains about Bethel, meaning to turn east there and cut through into the desert towards Mesopotamia.

The sun sank as he reached the hillside above Bethel, and he lay down to sleep leaning against a single great stone just below the top of the ridge.

Night fell, and as he slept Jacob dreamed. It seemed to him that a ladder stretched from earth to heaven before him with the angels —the Messengers of Jahveh—passing up and down it bringing Jahveh's messages to earth. And once more Jahveh promised him that his descendants would rule all the land and be spread through all the world, and that from them should come a blessing upon all mankind.

When Jacob woke his vision was so vivid in his mind that he knelt, saying:

'Surely this is the gateway of heaven where Jahveh dwells. Let this place be holy for ever more, and this stone against which I slept.'

Then he set up the stone like a pillar on the top of the ridge to mark the place, and for the first time called it Bethel, which means the House of God. And he made a vow, saying: 'If all that has been promised me indeed happens, then I swear to give a tenth part of all my possessions to Jahveh—and this tithe shall be his for ever more among my people.'

Jacob then went on his way, and came at length to Haran, where Laban now dwelt with all his family and followers.

Tired out with his journey, Jacob sat down beside a well and looked about him. The well had a great stone over its mouth, and three flocks of sheep were grazing round about it, as if waiting for their evening drink.

Presently the shepherds came in from either side, rolled the stone away and began to water their sheep.

'Friends, what place is this and where do you dwell?' asked Jacob.

'This is Haran,' they answered, 'and it is our home.'

'Do you know Laban, the son of Bethuel?' said Jacob.

'We do indeed,' they replied, 'and if you wait a little his daughter Rachel will be here with her father's sheep, for she herds them.'

Even as they spoke Rachel came driving the flock to water at the well. Then Jacob went up to her and helped her with the sheep. And after that he kissed her and told her who he was.

At once she sped into Haran and told her father; and Laban came running to welcome his nephew Jacob and to lead him to his house.

For a month Jacob dwelt with Laban as an honoured guest, But at the end of that time he said:

'My uncle, let me now serve you as a shepherd.'

But Laban said: 'Why, just because you are my sister's son, should you serve me for nothing? Tell me, what shall your wages be?'

Now Laban had two daughters. Leah the elder was tender-eyed; but the younger, Rachel, was beautiful and imposing—and Jacob had fallen in love with her at first sight by the well of Haran.

And he said to Laban: 'I will serve you for seven years for your daughter Rachel in marriage at the end of that time.'

'I had rather you married her than any other man,' said Laban, 'so I agree to your terms. Serve me seven years, and Rachel shall be yours.'

So Jacob served seven years to win Rachel, and they seemed to him no more than a few days, so great was his love.

When the seven years were completed Jacob said to Laban:

'I have earned my wife. Let me be wedded to Rachel as you promised.'

So Laban made a great feast to celebrate the wedding, with much food and wine. But when the night was come he veiled his elder daughter, Leah, and brought her to Jacob. And in the dimness of the bridal chamber, and after the wine that he had drunk, Jacob did not realize how he was being deceived.

But when day dawned and he awoke to find not Rachel but Leah beside him, he sprang up in a rage and rushed out to Laban.

'What is this that you have done to me!' he shouted. 'Did I not serve you for seven years to win Rachel? Why have you cheated me like this?'

And Laban answered: 'It is not lawful in our country for the younger daughter to be married before the elder. But now that you have married Leah all you need to do is to serve another seven years, and I will then give you Rachel to be your second wife.'

So Jacob worked for Laban for another seven years, and at the end of that time he married Rachel.

Now Leah, whom he loved less, bore him six sons and a daughter; but Rachel had no children, which made Jacob sad. Then he married two more wives, the handmaidens of Leah and Rachel, and they each bore him two sons.

He was still living at Haran and looking after Laban's flocks and herds; and in the twentieth year of his service Rachel at last bore him a son who was called Joseph.

Then Jacob rejoiced exceedingly, and decided that the time had come for him and his wives and children to set out for the land of Canaan so that as soon as his father Isaac was dead he could succeed him. For all this time Isaac, old and blind though he was, had still lingered on, tended by Rebekah and Esau.

When he decided to leave Haran Jacob demanded his share of Laban's flocks, and Laban was quite willing to divide them fairly. However, with his usual cunning Jacob was able to obtain by far the larger share, and he set out hastily for Canaan with them and his family on a day when Laban was away from home.

Following Jacob's example, Rachel stole her father's images which he valued more highly than anything he possessed. But she did not tell her husband what she had done.

When Laban returned home and found what had happened, he gathered his men together and set out in pursuit of Jacob.

He overtook him on Mount Gilead on the east of the Jordan valley, and it seemed at first that they would come to blows.

But Jacob was able to persuade him that he had only set out secretly so as to avoid the pain of parting after dwelling together for so long—and because he was afraid that Laban might try to keep Leah and Rachel.

'You may take your wives and children and the flocks and herds to Canaan,' said Laban, 'but not my sacred images which you have stolen from me.'

'I swear before Jahveh that I know nothing of your images,' said Jacob. 'Search my camp, and if you find them slay that man or woman in whose tent they are.'

So Laban searched everywhere, and came at last to the tent where his daughter Rachel was. Now she had hidden the images among the rugs which were spread on her camel's back when she was riding it. She was sitting on this heap of rugs when Laban came to her tent, and she said:

'Father, pardon me for not rising to greet you. I am not well, for the sickness that women have has fallen upon me.'

So Laban searched the whole tent; but he did not seek among the rugs on which Rachel sat.

Therefore he found no images and when he returned to him Jacob reproached him, saying:

'Why do you try to find a reason to quarrel with me? I have served you faithfully for twenty years, and won your daughters to be my wives by honest labour. And by honest labour I have earned my share of the flocks and herds—for under my care they grew and increased as never before.'

Then Laban made peace with Jacob; and they kissed and embraced and wept at parting. And Laban and all his followers returned to Haran.

When he had gone Rachel jumped up and ran out to Jacob and told him how she had stolen the images and prevented Laban from finding them. And they rejoiced together at having cheated Laban so cleverly and brought away such riches with them.

But now they had to meet a greater danger. For Laban sent messengers to Esau telling him how Jacob had treated him and, as he hoped, Esau's hatred of his brother broke out into violent threats. And he gathered an army of four hundred men and set out to attack him.

Jacob heard of this, and he divided his people into two parties, sending one ahead under Eliezer, bidding him meet Esau in peace and give him many rich gifts, and say that he, Jacob, came in peace also.

Then Jacob set out with his wives and children by a different route, and led them to another ford of the torrent called Jabbok which runs from Gilead down into the Jordan, and which he must cross to reach the land of Canaan.

All day Jacob's followers crossed the Jabbok, and when night fell only he remained on the north bank.

As he came down to the ford a strange man barred his way, saying:

'You cannot pass this way unless you wrestle with me.'

So Jacob threw off his robe and wrestled with the stranger. But, strong though he was, he could not overthrow him.

All night they wrestled, and when day began to break the stranger touched Jacob on the thigh—and at once the sinew shrank and a bone in Jacob's leg went out of joint.

But Jacob still gripped the stranger and would not admit defeat, and at last the stranger said:

'Let me go, for the day is breaking.'

'I will not let you go unless you give me your blessing,' said Jacob.

'What is your name?' asked the stranger.

'Jacob,' was the answer.

'You shall no more be called Jacob,' said the stranger, 'but henceforth you are Israel, and your descendants shall be called

Isaac blessed Esau and Jacob

the Children of Israel, and this land shall be called Israel after you. You have proved yourself to be a "Prince of Jahveh"—for that is what the name "Israel" means.'

'And who are you who tell me this?' asked Jacob.

'There is no need to ask my name,' answered the stranger. And he blessed Jacob, and straightway vanished.

Then Jacob knew that he had wrestled with an angel, a Messenger of Jahveh, and he called that ford of the Jabbok 'Penuel', which means 'the Face of Jahveh', for he said: 'I have here looked upon the strength of Jahveh, and yet my life is preserved and Jahveh's promise has come true.'

After this Jacob crossed the Jabbok by the ford of Penuel and led his wives and children down fearlessly towards the Jordan.

There Esau met him, and Jahveh turned his rage to love so that he ran forward and flung his arms round Jacob and kissed him and wept.

Thus the two brothers were reconciled, and Jacob and the Children of Israel settled down peacefully in the land of Canaan and dwelt there happily for a number of years.

But first of all the two brothers visited Isaac, who blessed them before he died. And when he was dead they buried him and mourned long at his grave.

After this they divided the land, and Israel, who had been Jacob, dwelt at Bethel where he had seen the vision of the ladder leading up to heaven.

JOSEPH AND HIS BROTHERS

For a long time Joseph was the youngest of Jacob's sons, and Jacob loved him better than all the rest. As a sign of his especial love he made for him a coat of many colours, and he continued to shower favours on him, even after the birth of his twelfth and youngest son Benjamin. For Rachel died in giving birth to Benjamin, and with her last breath gave him that name, which means 'child of sorrow'.

The more favour Jacob showed to Joseph, the more jealous his other sons grew of their young brother, until at last their jealousy turned to hatred and all of them except Reuben, the eldest, began to plot his death.

They were more particularly tempted to remove Joseph because one day when he was seventeen he dreamed a strange dream, and—since messages from Jahveh were thought to come in dreams—he felt no hesitation in telling it to them.

'Listen to my dream,' he said. 'I dreamed that we were all harvesting the corn and binding up the sheaves in the field, when suddenly my sheaf stood upright all by itself. And lo and behold! your sheaves gathered round and bowed down to my sheaf and promised to obey it.'

'You mean that you are going to rule over us?' growled his brothers angrily. '*You* have dominion over *us*? What an idea!'

So they hated him all the more—and more still when he had another dream, which he told to them and also this time to Jacob.

'I have dreamed another and a stranger dream,' said Joseph. 'In it the sun and the moon and the eleven brightest stars bowed down and promised to obey me.'

Jacob scolded him, saying: 'What sort of dream is this to have?

Do you really believe that your mother and I, and your eleven brothers, will ever bow down before you and offer our services?'

Jacob thought over this dream, however, for he felt that it might indeed come from Jahveh and hold some hidden meaning.

But Joseph's brothers merely hated him all the more, and looked out for a chance to murder him without anyone discovering their guilt.

Their chance came one day when they were tending their father's sheep at Shechem, among the fertile valleys to the west of Jordan, which in later days was called Samaria.

Jacob called for Joseph and said: 'Your brothers have been a long time away. Go now to Shechem and see if all is well with them and with the flocks, and bring me word.'

So Joseph, clad in his coat of many colours, set out through the Vale of Hebron and into Shechem. Finally he found his brothers on the hillside of Dothan.

As he came down the long slope towards them, one said to another: 'See where our dreamer comes!'

And they began to plot, saying: 'This is our chance to kill Joseph and throw his body into some pit. We can tell our father that a wild beast has eaten him. Then we shall see what truth there is in his dreams!'

Reuben heard his brothers making these plans, and he said: 'If we shed our brother's blood, the guilt of it will bring a curse upon us. So let us put him into the pit over there without hurting him.'

This he said, intending to come back later and rescue Joseph. But his brothers thought that he was to be left there to die of starvation, and they agreed eagerly.

So when Joseph reached his brothers they seized him, tore off his coat of many colours and threw him into the pit. There was no water in it at the time, so he took no harm; but it was deep, and its sides were sheer, and he could not climb out.

Later in the day, while Reuben was away, the fourth brother, Judah, noticed a caravan of Ishmaelites—a wandering tribe of Bedouins—approaching across the desert.

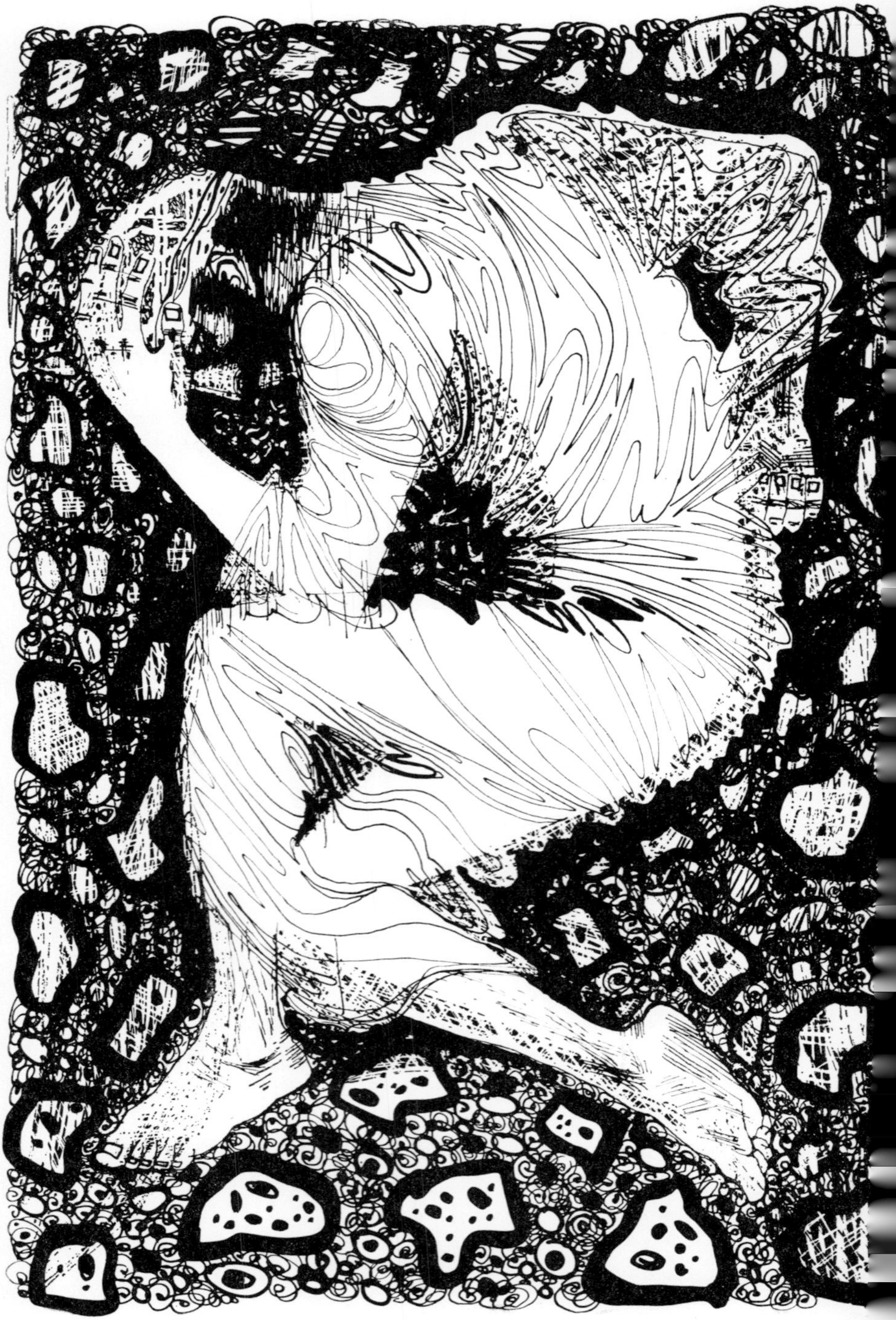

'Listen!' he exclaimed to his brothers. 'Even if we leave Joseph to starve in the pit we shall be guilty of his blood—and that is a bad thing to risk. But if we take him and sell him to these Ishmaelites we are doing no harm. And they will take him with them wherever they are going, and sell him as a slave.'

This seemed a splendid idea; and his brothers dragged Joseph out of the pit and sold him as a slave for twenty pieces of silver to the Ishmaelites—who were delighted to have so fine a young man to sell at Joppa or Tanis to the Phoenicians or the Egyptians or the seafarers from Crete.

When Reuben came back and found that Joseph was no longer in the pit, he tore his clothes in sorrow and wept for the loss of his brother.

But the rest of them killed a kid and dipped Joseph's coat of many colours in the blood. Then they carried it to Jacob and said:

'See what we have found! Surely it cannot be Joseph's coat?'

But Jacob recognized it at once, and wailed: 'It is! It is! It is the coat of many colours that I made for my beloved. Joseph is certainly torn in pieces and eaten by wild beasts!'

Then he tore his clothes, and dressed himself in sackcloth and mourned and lamented. His daughter Dinah and his sons tried in vain to comfort him; but Jacob refused to be comforted, saying: 'I will mourn for my son Joseph until I die, so that I may go down into my grave to join him still mourning.'

But Joseph was not dead. The Ishmaelites failed to get a good price for him at Joppa; so they took him down the coast into Lower Egypt, and at Tanis in the Delta, which at that time was the capital, they sold him to an Egyptian called Potiphar, who was the Captain of Pharaoh's Guard and Chamberlain of his Court.

As Joseph grew into a handsome young man, he found great favour with Potiphar, who trusted him in everything, and finally made him overseer of his household. For everything that Joseph

They threw him into the pit

did seemed to prosper, and Potiphar felt sure that this noble stranger from the land of Canaan was one favoured by the gods.

At last, however, Joseph's charm proved his undoing. For Potiphar's wife Zelicha fell in love with him, and began to pester him to return her affection.

Joseph, however, was too honest to take advantage of her wicked passion.

'Potiphar, my master, trusts me absolutely,' he said, 'and I cannot betray his trust. Moreover if I did this great wickedness, it would be a sin against the commandments of Jahveh, the one God whom I worship. And surely too your Egyptian gods forbid such a thing also—Amen-Ra and Isis and Osiris and the rest.'

But Zelicha cared nothing for the gods, either of Egypt or of Israel, and continued to tempt Joseph until one day her love turned to hatred—or to fear lest he should tell the truth to Potiphar—and she tore her clothes and rushed shrieking to her husband saying that Joseph had insulted and assaulted her.

Then Potiphar, believing his wife's lies, took Joseph and cast him into prison. And there he remained for twelve years, though Zelicha came to visit him from time to time offering to procure his liberty if only he would run away with her.

In time she gave up pestering Joseph, and the affair was forgotten. But Joseph lived quite happily in the royal prison, for he soon became a favourite of the governor's, who made him his second in command and let him look after the other prisoners.

It happened one day that two important prisoners were brought into the prison, and Joseph was put in charge of them. These were Pharaoh's Chief Butler and Chief Baker, and they were sent to prison because at a great feast Pharaoh's guests found dead flies in the wine which the butler poured out and fragments of stone in the bread which the baker had made.

One morning when Joseph came to visit the two prisoners he found them looking very sad. He asked them if they were in any pain or anxiety, and the butler answered: 'Last night each of us dreamed strange dreams which we are sure were sent to us by

Amen-Ra. But we cannot tell what they mean, for there is no *kharthibi*, no interpreter of dreams in the prison.'

'The meanings of dreams are shown to those to whom the god wishes to reveal them,' said Joseph. 'Therefore tell me your dreams, and perhaps Jahveh, whom I worship, may show the meanings of them to me.'

'In my dream', said the butler, 'I saw before me a vine with three branches. It was as though it budded, and the blossoms opened as I watched, and the grapes grew and ripened in a moment. Pharaoh's cup was in my hand, and I picked the grapes and squeezed their juice into the cup and gave it to Pharaoh.'

'The three branches are three days,' said Joseph. 'In three days Pharaoh will forgive you and restore you to your place, and you will be his Chief Butler once more and fill his wine-cup for him. That is the meaning of your dream; and I beg you, when it comes true, do not forget me, but ask Pharaoh to take me out of prison. For I am shut up here on a false charge and have been here for ten years—I was born free in the land of Canaan and sold as a slave into Egypt.'

It was now the baker's turn to tell his dream, and he said: 'It seemed to me that I had three white baskets on my head, and the top one was full of bread and cakes which I had made for Pharaoh —but the birds came and ate them all.'

'The three baskets are three days also,' said Joseph. 'In three days Pharaoh shall take you out of prison—but it will be to hang you on a tree where the birds shall come and eat your flesh off your bones.'

Three days after this Pharaoh held a great feast to celebrate his birthday, and he sent for the Chief Butler and restored him to favour and bade him fill his wine-cup as of old.

As for the baker, he commanded his servants to take him and hang him from a tree, just as Joseph had said would happen.

But the Chief Butler forgot all about his promise to Joseph, and left him to languish in the prison for two years more.

At the end of that time, however, Pharaoh himself began to dream—two dreams, one after the other in the same night. And he was so troubled by his dreams that he sent for all the *kharthibis* and wise men and magicians of Egypt to interpret them; but none could tell him what his dreams meant.

Then suddenly the Chief Butler struck himself upon the head and cried: 'O Pharaoh, life, health, strength be to you, I remember my faults this day! Two full years ago when I lay in prison under your just displeasure, the Chief Baker and I each dreamed a dream: and there was a young man from the land of Canaan who served the governor of the prison, though he was himself a prisoner, who interpreted our dreams and read them truly. For things happened exactly as he told us our dreams showed that they would: the Chief Baker was hanged, and I was restored to my place in your royal household.'

Immediately Pharaoh sent to the prison for Joseph. And after he had shaved and washed and put on a fine robe which was sent to him, he came before Pharaoh, and bowed low before him.

And Pharaoh said to Joseph: 'I have dreamed a dream, and none of my *kharthibis*, the interpreters of dreams, nor of my wise men, nor of my magicians, can tell me what it means. But I have been told that you are skilled in reading the messages sent to us in dreams.'

Joseph answered Pharaoh: 'It is no skill of mine; but if Jahveh, whom I worship, chooses to speak through my lips, then I can bring peace to Pharaoh's mind.'

And Pharaoh said: 'In my dream I stood upon the bank of the River Nile, and there came up out of the river seven cows who were fat and healthy, and they fed in the meadow near by. But then seven more cows came up out of the river, and they were lean and ill, and their bones stuck out—they were cattle such as I have never seen in all the land of Egypt. And as I watched the lean cows ate up the fat ones—yet when they had done so you could never have guessed it, for they were still as thin and miserable as before.

'This dream had scarcely ended when I found myself in the midst of another. This time I saw seven ears of corn coming up and ripening out of one stalk, and they were fine and full and golden. Then there came up seven more ears out of one corn stalk, but these were withered and thin and blasted by the wind. Yet the thin ears ate up the good ears, and were none the fatter for so doing.

'All these things I have told to my magicians and wise men and *kharthibis*, but none of them can tell me what they mean.'

Then Joseph said: 'The two dreams which Pharaoh has dreamed are one dream. In it Jahveh has shown Pharaoh what he is about to do. The seven fat cows and the seven good ears of corn are seven years of plenty; and the seven lean cows and seven empty ears of corn are seven years also: they are seven years of famine.

'What this means is that the next seven years will be years of great plenty throughout Egypt; but after them shall come seven years of famine when the Nile will not rise and the harvests shall wither or not grow at all. It will be seven years of starvation.

'Now my advice is that since Jahveh—or the gods of Egypt—have warned Pharaoh of what is to come, that he chooses a wise and honest man and gives him power throughout all Egypt to appoint overseers who shall take a fifth part of all the crops that ripen during the seven years of plenty. And let him store the fifth part taken during the years of plenty so that there shall be food in Egypt during the seven years of famine, and the people shall not starve.'

Joseph's advice seemed good and wise to Pharaoh and his advisers, but they said: 'Where can we find such a man who will use such great powers honestly and wisely?'

Pharaoh turned at once to Joseph and said: 'Since the gods have shown you all this, it seems to me that we are likely to find no one else so honest and discreet and wise. Therefore I set you over Egypt to be my viceroy and to carry out this my will. All people in Egypt shall obey you, and only I shall be greater than you are.'

Then Pharaoh took off his own royal ring with his royal cartouche on it, and set it on Joseph's finger, saying: 'See, I give you rule over all Egypt!'

After this Joseph was dressed in rich garments with a gold chain round his neck and was driven through the streets of Tanis in a chariot that came second only to that of Pharaoh; and he was proclaimed Pharaoh's viceroy with powers equal to those of Pharaoh himself, through all Lower Egypt from the cities of the Delta to Memphis by the great Pyramids, and upstream towards Thebes itself.

Then Joseph was given an Egyptian name, 'Tche-pa-nete-auf-ankh', which means 'The god spoke and he came into life'; and Pharaoh gave him as head wife the Princess Nes-Neth, daughter of the Prince of Heliopolis; and he became the ruler of Egypt.

For the next seven years he travelled hither and thither through the land seeing that the corn was gathered up and stored away in the royal granaries during the seven years of plenty. And indeed they were years such as had never been known in Egypt since the golden age when Ra, the father of the gods, reigned upon earth. Joseph gathered in the golden grain as if it had been sea sand, so plenteous was it—and very soon he ceased to count how many bushels were claimed for the royal granaries, for there was such abundance that it could not be numbered.

In the eighth year the Nile did not rise sufficiently to cover the land with the rich mud in which the crops grew so well, and there was a great drought in Egypt and in the countries near by—in Palestine and Syria and Mesopotamia.

When the Egyptians had used up all their own stores of grain, and the next year's inundation showed every sign of leaving the land once more without a harvest, they began to starve. And when the famine grew keen they cried to Pharaoh for bread; and Pharaoh sent out his commands: 'Go to Joseph and do all that he bids you!'

Then Joseph opened the royal granaries and doled out to the people of Egypt so that there was no hunger among them any more. But he kept back not only enough corn for the rest of the seven lean years, but also a great deal more which he began to sell at a high price to the people of the other lands who were hit by the famine and who soon came to know that there was corn in Egypt, if nowhere else.

The famine struck that part of Palestine where Jacob and the Children of Israel dwelt among the Canaanites as hard as anywhere else. In the second year of it Jacob's sons came to him in their trouble, and he said to them:
  'Why do you look so anxious? Listen. I have heard that there is corn in Egypt. Go there and buy enough to last us until next harvest—for otherwise we shall starve.'
  So Jacob's ten elder sons set out for Egypt. But he would not let Benjamin go with them, saying: 'He is my youngest, a mere boy. Let him stay with me, for if evil should befall him there would be no comfort left to me now that Joseph is dead.'
  So the ten brothers took money and beasts of burden and set out for Egypt to buy corn. When they arrived there they were led before Joseph, together with many others who had come from the lands which were stricken by famine who also hoped to buy food.
  Now Joseph was dressed as a great lord of Egypt, and his brothers did not recognize him—for indeed he had been only a boy when they sold him into slavery, and most of them thought that he was probably dead long ago.
  But Joseph recognized his brothers at once when they came and knelt before him to beg for corn. However, he showed no sign; instead he glared at them haughtily, and spoke to them through an interpreter, pretending that he could speak only Egyptian and did not understand Hebrew.
  'Where do you come from?' he demanded.
  'From the land of Canaan,' they answered. 'We come to buy food, for the famine is cruel in Canaan, and we will die if we cannot get corn.'
  Joseph thought of his dreams, and of all that had happened since then, and he glared at his kneeling brothers and said:
  'I do not believe your lying tales. You are spies come to see how Egypt may most easily be attacked, and where her defences are weakest.'

'Indeed, my lord, that is not so!' they cried. 'We are the sons of one man, and not spies of the Canaanites.'

'A likely tale!' sneered Joseph. 'All of you the sons of one Canaanite?'

'There were twelve of us,' said Reuben. 'One is dead, and the youngest has remained at home with our father Jacob, who is an old man, whose wife is dead, and who needs the comfort of the young son of his old age.'

'I still say that you are spies, and all this is a lying tale woven to deceive me,' said Joseph. 'Therefore, if you want me to believe you, prove your words by sending one of you to fetch this young brother of whom you speak. As for the rest of you, I'll have you locked up in prison until he comes. I'll give you three days to think about my words—three days which all ten of you shall spend in Pharaoh's prison.'

So for three days the brothers were shut up in the prison where Joseph had once been confined. And at the end of that time he came to them and said:

'I will let all but one of you go, so that you may carry corn back to your father and your families. But one I shall keep here in prison until you return bringing your youngest brother with you.'

Then they were much troubled, and said to one another: 'Surely Jahveh is punishing us now for having no mercy on Joseph when we had bound him and thrown him into the pit, and not heeding his prayers and tears when we sold him to the Ishmaelites as a slave.'

'Did I not warn you?' said Reuben. 'Joseph's blood is on our heads, and we must suffer the penalty.'

Now Joseph was listening to this, though he was still pretending that he understood no Hebrew; and when he heard their words he turned away and wept secretly. But presently he turned again and spoke harshly in Egyptian, his words being translated to them by the interpreter.

'Take yonder Canaanite,' he commanded, pointing to Simeon, the second brother. 'Bind him and shut him up in the prison cell.

But fill these other men's sacks with corn and let them set out at once for Canaan.'

Then he spoke privately to the men who were taking the sacks to fill, saying: 'In each sack place the money which these men brought with them to pay for the corn. Do not let them see what you have done, but lace up the sacks tightly and set them on the beasts of burden ready for the journey.'

The servants did as they were commanded, and presently the nine sons of Jacob were riding over the desert in the direction of Canaan.

On the way one of them happened to open his sack to give some corn to his ass, and found the money with which he had paid for it right on top of the corn. At this they all looked in their sacks and found their own money, and were filled with fear, for they thought that Pharaoh's viceroy had done this so as to have an excuse to arrest them as thieves and cheats.

However, they got safely back to Canaan and told Jacob everything that had happened to them. Then Jacob wept and lamented, saying: 'First I must lose Joseph; and now Simeon is a prisoner in Egypt; and on top of all this you want to take Benjamin away from me. No, you shall *not* take him—for if anything happens to Benjamin, you will bring down my grey hairs with sorrow to the grave.'

None the less the following year when the famine continued the sons of Israel saw that they and their wives and children would die of starvation unless they bought more grain in Egypt. And they knew that to Pharaoh and to Pharaoh's viceroy they could not return unless they took Benjamin with them.

At last Jacob realized that there was no other way and, after begging them to take special care of Benjamin, he said:

'Since it must be so, go now and quickly. But take with you the best produce of this land in your sacks as a present to Pharaoh's viceroy: a little balm, a little honey, spices and myrrh, nuts and almonds. And take not only double money, but also that which you took last year and found in your sacks—in case it was put there by accident. Now take Benjamin, and go! And may Jahveh watch over you and bring you safely back to me, together with Benjamin and Simeon.'

So the sons of Israel set out once more for Egypt, and in due time came to Tanis and were ushered into Joseph's presence where he sat dispensing corn from Pharaoh's barns and granaries.

When he saw them, and that they had brought Benjamin, he said to his steward:

'Bring these men to my house, for they shall dine with me today. And make sure that a great feast is prepared for them.'

Reuben and his brothers were filled with fear when they found themselves being led off to the viceroy's palace, for they thought that they were there to be seized for stealing the last year's purchase money and cast into a dungeon.

However, the steward reassured them, saying that he had full records of having received their money for the corn which they had bought the previous year. And he led them into the palace where slaves attended to them, washing their feet and bringing them scented water in which to dip their hands.

When Joseph came home at noon his brothers bowed down before him and gave him the presents which Jacob had told them to bring. And Joseph received them graciously, asking: 'I trust that the old man your father, of whom you told me, is well?' And, when he saw Benjamin: 'Is this your youngest brother whom you were to bring to prove that you told no lying tale?'

As soon as he was assured that it was indeed Benjamin, Joseph sent for Simeon, who had been kept as a hostage, though treated as a guest rather than as a prisoner. Then Joseph led them into the feast; but before they sat down he took in his hands a great silver cup set with jewels, and when it had been filled with wine he said:

'You have heard of the magic of the Egyptians: see now I will gaze into this cup and tell each of you his name in order of birth so that you may sit at my table in due seniority. The eldest is called Reuben: there he stands, and there is the seat prepared for him.'

So Joseph went through them all in order, and they marvelled at the magic of the Egyptians. At the last he said: 'The eleventh is called Joseph—and he you say is dead or a slave. So I will take his place and sit here next to the youngest, Benjamin: for he has no mother living, and neither have I!'

They feasted and drank until nightfall, and still none of them had the least idea that Pharaoh's viceroy was their brother Joseph. And when they were asleep Joseph said to his steward:

'Fill their sacks with corn, and in each put the money they have paid for it. But in the sack of Benjamin the youngest place also my great silver cup.'

Next morning the eleven brothers found the sacks already loaded on to their pack-animals, so they set off in the direction of Canaan, hoping that they were all now safely escaped out of Egypt.

But Joseph had not done with them. As soon as they were well away into the desert he gave careful orders to his steward, who set out after them with a troop of well-armed men.

He overtook them half a day's journey from Tanis and roughly bade them stand, saying: 'Why have you rewarded evil for good? You have stolen the great silver cup from which our lord the viceroy Tche-pa-nete-auf-ankh drinks and in which he sees visions.'

Reuben and the rest denied this charge vigorously, saying: 'Search and see that we have done no such thing. And if you find the silver cup, then do what you will to him in whose sack it lies.'

But when the steward found it in Benjamin's sack they tore their clothes in despair, and insisted on accompanying him back to the viceroy's palace.

Here Judah knelt before Joseph and said: 'My lord, we do not know how this thing happened. But both last year and this our money was in our sacks with the corn—and this time the silver cup was there also, though none of us placed it there.'

'Benjamin who stole the cup remains here as my slave,' said Joseph. 'The rest of you may go.'

'I beg you to let him go and keep me in his place,' said Judah.

'Slay me, do what you will to me—but let Benjamin go. For I promised my father Jacob to bring him back in safety.'

Then Joseph could keep up the pretence no longer. He sent all the Egyptians out of the room, and cried aloud in Hebrew:

'My brothers! My brothers! Do you not know me? I am Joseph, your brother! Joseph whom you sold as a slave into Egypt! See, my dreams have come true and you have all bowed down before me. But now I forgive you for the evil you intended, since such good has come out of it. You shall return to Canaan immediately and tell my father that Jahveh has made me the master of all Egypt. Tell Jacob to come hither with all his people, and come all of you with your wives and families, and I will give you rich lands in Egypt, and Egypt shall be yours and you shall rule over it as I do!'

ISRAEL IN EGYPT

When Joseph had made himself known to his brothers and shown that he had forgiven them for their plot against him, he loaded them with gifts and sent them back to Canaan to fetch Jacob and all their families.

With their asses laden with corn and bread and other good things from Egypt, they crossed the desert into Palestine and drew near to Canaan.

As they approached Jacob's tents they said one to another: 'How shall we break this news to our father? If we tell him suddenly that Joseph is alive and has become the ruler of Egypt, the shock may be too much for so old a man.'

But it chanced that Serach, the daughter of Asher, the eighth brother, came to meet them. Now she was famed for her singing, and she played very sweetly on the harp. So they said to her:

'Take your harp and go and sit before our father as your custom is. Play to him, as you do so often, and sing to him. But in your song tell him that his son Joseph lives, and so break the news to him gently.'

Serach did as they told her and went to sing to her grandfather. And the chorus of her song, which came seven times, ran:

> Joseph, escaped from snare and guile
> Now lives and rules beside the Nile.

Jacob was delighted with the song, though he did not fully believe the words of it. But while she was assuring him that they were true, his sons arrived leading the laden asses and knelt before him, saying:

'We come with joyful tidings indeed. Joseph, our brother, is

They set out on the long trek into Egypt

still alive. He has prospered greatly and is now ruler over all the land of Egypt.'

Still Jacob would not believe the good news. But when they showed him all the presents that Joseph had sent his eyes brightened and gladness sparkled in their depths, and he exclaimed:

'Now I know that Joseph is indeed alive—and I will go and see him before I die.'

So he gathered together all his family: his sons and his grandsons and all their wives and women and children. And they gathered their flocks and herds and all their goods, and set out on the long trek into Egypt—more than three hundred miles, first through the mountains of Palestine, and then by the north of the Desert of Sinai into the Egyptian Delta near the Salt Lakes on the Isthmus of Suez, and to the Land of Goshen to the south of Tanis which Joseph had set apart for them.

Jacob sent Judah in advance to announce his coming, and when Joseph knew of it he gathered together his friends and followers and a great army of Egyptians who were under his command. They were clad in rich garments with gold and silver ornaments, and the troops were fully armed as if for war. Music and gladness filled the land, and all the people, the women and the children gathered on the house tops to watch the magnificent procession.

Joseph was dressed in royal robes, with the crown of Egypt upon his head; but when he drew near to his father he stepped down from his chariot and walked to meet him. And when the nobles and princes saw this they too descended from their horses and chariots and walked with him.

When Jacob saw all this great procession he was amazed and said to Judah: 'Who is this great king who comes to meet us at the head of so splendid an array?'

And Judah answered: 'That is your son Joseph!'

Then Joseph and Jacob ran into each other's arms and kissed and embraced and wept. And Jacob said:

'Now I am ready to die. I have seen the face of my beloved son, who I thought was dead, living and the ruler of a rich land.'

So Joseph led Israel and the children of Israel to the rich land of Goshen, and they settled there and were welcomed by Pharaoh and his people. And Jacob became the great lord Ya-kob-her, and he and Joseph were the first of the Hyksōs or 'chieftains from the foreign hills'. But afterwards, when the Egyptians came to hate them, they called Israel and his children the Aamu, 'the Asiatics'.

At first, however, the Israelites were welcomed by the Egyptians, and Joseph led Jacob to visit Pharaoh, accompanied by five of his brothers.

Before entering Pharaoh's presence Joseph warned them, saying: 'The people of Egypt have no great love for shepherds: therefore say little about your flocks, but much about your herds of cattle and your skill in breeding and tending them.'

Then he led them in, and Pharaoh welcomed Jacob, who called down a blessing on him.

Presently Pharaoh asked: 'What is your occupation, and why have you come into the land of Egypt?'

Jacob answered: 'We have come with our flocks and herds because of the famine which is particularly severe in the land of Canaan—and we beg that you will let us pitch our tents and feed our beasts in Goshen until such time as we can return home. My sons are skilled breeders and herders of cattle, and will serve you all they can.'

'All Goshen lies open to you,' said Pharaoh, 'and I will make the most skilled among you the ruler over my herds of cattle. For your son Joseph has saved Egypt from great suffering and has brought wealth to the land—and another son of yours may bring still greater prosperity if my cattle are under his care.'

So Jacob and the Children of Israel settled in Goshen, and Joseph heaped riches upon them and gave them as much bread as they could possibly need.

But the famine grew more sore for the Egyptians, and they came to Joseph to buy corn until all their money was spent. And after that they traded their cattle for more corn, and then their lands and then their own persons.

Then Joseph said to them: 'Now I have bought you and your land for Pharaoh, and henceforth you and your children for ever shall pay a fifth part of your income to him—and I will give you seed to sow, and next year corn will grow once more in the land of Egypt.'

Joseph also settled most of the Egyptians in cities, since now the corn lands belonged to Pharaoh and not to them, they had become his servants who planted his crops and reaped his harvests rather than their own.

Only the priests escaped from this servitude, since Pharaoh made them special gifts of corn each year. And also the Children of Israel to whom Joseph gave all that they needed. And when the years of famine were ended they remained in Goshen, showing no signs of wishing to return to Canaan.

Jacob lived for seventeen years after coming to Egypt, and died at the age of a hundred and forty-seven.

As he lay on his deathbed he called all his sons before him and blessed them. He also prophesied, telling each of them what parts of Palestine their descendants would rule when at length they returned to the Promised Land and became the Twelve Tribes of Israel.

At the last he begged Joseph not to bury him in Egypt but to carry his body back to Canaan and bury it in the cave by Mamre where Abraham and Sarah and Isaac and Rebekah and his own wife Leah already lay.

So when he was dead, Joseph had his body embalmed in the Egyptian manner; and he and his brothers carried it to the cave in Canaan. But when the funeral was completed they returned to Egypt and continued to dwell in Goshen.

Joseph lived to the age of a hundred and ten. And as he lay dying with his children and grandchildren and great-grandchildren about him he said:

'The time will come when Jahveh will bring you out of Egypt into the Promised Land of Canaan. Therefore, when I am dead, embalm my body and keep it by you to carry back to Mamre when the time comes for your exodus out of Egypt.'

When they had sworn Joseph died. And his body was embalmed and placed in a coffin in Egypt, and kept unburied until the appointed day.

Book Three

THE ESCAPE OUT OF EGYPT

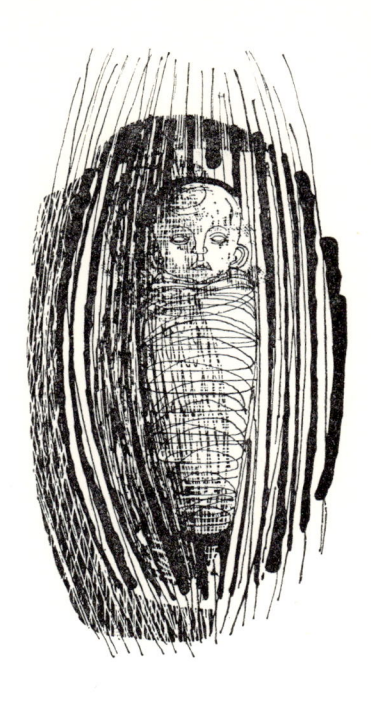

THE ADVENTURES OF MOSES

The years passed, and the Children of Israel still dwelt in the land of Egypt, growing and multiplying until from a family they became a nation, and the land was filled with them.

About fifty years after Joseph's death, when his services at the time of the great famine were more or less forgotten, the Egyptians began to grow anxious about these strangers who were becoming as numerous as themselves.

The Pharaoh of that day did not know how to deal with this growing population of aliens, and he said to his counsellors:
'We must take steps to prevent these Israelite shepherds from

becoming too powerful. For already if it came to war, and they attacked us, they might easily be the victors.'

And so, to prove that they were servants and not masters, and to keep down their numbers by persecution, Pharaoh set taskmasters over the Israelites who made them labour hard building the citadels of Ramses and Pi-Aten to guard the land of Goshen.

However, the more they were made to work and to suffer, the faster the numbers of the Israelites grew, and the more frightened the Egyptians became of having their country altogether overrun by them.

So Pharaoh passed further laws against the Israelites, and finally decreed that any sons born to them should be thrown into the Nile, though the daughters should be allowed to live.

Not long after the passing of this harsh law a young man called Amram, who was a grandson of Jacob's third son Levi, married one of his cousins whose name was Jochebed. When a son was born to them they could not bear to throw him into the river and so Jochebed tended him in secret.

When the child was three months old, however, Jochebed could hide him no longer. So she made a tiny ark out of bulrushes, daubed it with pitch so as to keep out the water, put the baby in it and let it float along the bank of the Nile near where the city of Cairo now stands.

Jochebed dared not remain near the ark, but her daughter Miriam, who was still only a child, played among the reeds on the river's edge—but kept an eye on the floating cradle in which her baby brother lay.

Now it chanced that Merrhis, the daughter of Pharaoh, came down from her father's palace in the nearby city of Heliopolis to bathe in the Nile and play ball with her slave-girls on the bank.

She saw the ark floating on the water, and bade them bring it to her. When she looked inside and found a beautiful baby boy she was delighted.

'This must be the child of one of the Israelites from Goshen,' she said. 'It is such a lovely baby, and holds out its arms to me so trustfully, that I shall keep it and bring it up as if it were my own.'

THE ADVENTURES OF MOSES

Presently Miriam came wandering along the bank, and the Princess Merrhis called to her: 'Girl, you are surely one of these Israelites? I have found this baby of your race and I want a nurse to suckle and tend him; can you find me an Israelitish woman who will do so?'

At once Miriam went off and fetched the child's mother Jochebed, who readily agreed to be its nurse.

And so the baby, whom Merrhis named Moses, which means 'drawn out of the water' in the language of the Israelites, was taken to live in Pharaoh's palace, and was brought up as a prince of Egypt.

He was a clever child—so clever that he nearly met his end at the age of three. Pharaoh was sitting at his banquet table one day, with his queen on one side and on the other his daughter Merrhis, who had Moses on her knee. Suddenly the little boy reached up, snatched the royal crown from Pharaoh's head and placed it on his own.

The people cried out in horror, and Pharaoh, fearing that this was an evil omen, turned to his chief magician Bilam and said:

'Tell me what this means—and how the child should be punished.'

'O Pharaoh, life, health, strength be to you,' answered Bilam, 'do not imagine that because the child is young he did this thing without thought. The spirit of understanding is already in this child, and he seeks to take your kingdom wholly to himself. Such has always been the way of his people, the Israelites, both among themselves, as when Jacob cheated Esau of his birthright, and since Joseph came to Egypt a century and a half ago. Remember how he brought all his family to feed upon the substance of Egypt while the Egyptians were forced to sell themselves to him in exchange for corn. This child is following Joseph's example, and would take the very crown from you; therefore I say let his blood be spilled so that Egypt may be saved from him.'

Then Merrhis wept and begged for the child's life, saying: 'He is only a baby and did not know what he did. The crown shone and glittered, and he reached out his hand to take it thinking it no more than a plaything.'

Then another of Pharaoh's advisers, Jethro, a priest of Midian, said: 'O Pharaoh, life, health, strength be to you, let us test this matter and see whether the child is yet of an age to think and reason. Bring two bowls, one containing fire and the other gold, and set them before him. If he takes the gold, then slay him; but if he grasps at the fire, which is brighter, then spare his life.'

Pharaoh approved of this, and the two bowls were brought and set before the child. But Moses, realizing his danger, snatched at the fire and crammed it into his mouth, burning his tongue badly, and from that day on becoming 'heavy of mouth and heavy of tongue'.

So his life was saved, and he grew up a handsome lad, and was dressed as a prince and honoured by the people. When he was old enough he was sent to the temple at Heliopolis, where he learned all the wisdom of the priests. Here he was given the Egyptian name of Osar-seph, and made a member of the priesthood.

But he remained faithful to his own people, and indeed spent much time in Goshen learning all that had happened to his ancestors before his birth, and how they had come to Egypt, and what they had suffered in recent years.

Then Moses tried to ease their burdens by asking Pharaoh to deal more kindly with them. But Pharaoh and his advisers were growing more and more frightened of these colonists who were spreading over Egypt and threatening by their numbers to occupy the whole of the Lower Kingdom—and the utmost Moses could gain for them was that they should rest from their labours for one day in each week. And even this he was able to gain for them only by pointing out that a day's rest would allow them to renew their strength to labour harder for Pharaoh's profit.

When Moses was about eighteen years old he chanced one day to be wandering in Goshen, and he saw an Egyptian overseer beating an Israelite workman who was one of his own cousins. Then a great rage surged up in his heart and, having looked this way and that to be sure that no one could see them, Moses drew

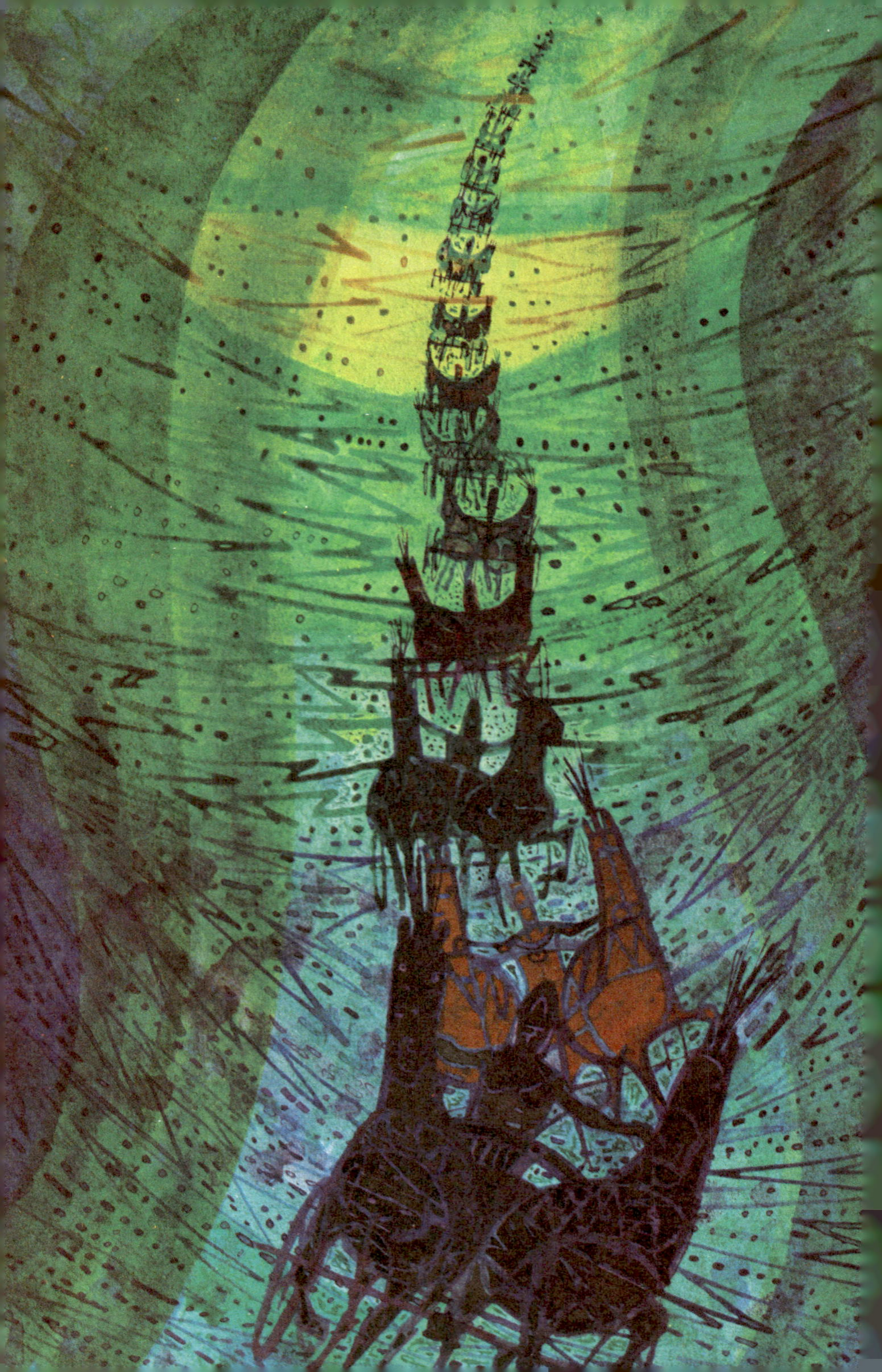

his sword and killed the Egyptian, burying his body deep in the sand so as to leave no trace.

Next day, however, as he wandered again in Goshen, Moses chanced upon two Israelites quarrelling and fighting with each other. He strove to settle their difference, but the man who was to blame shouted:

'Who made you a prince and a judge over us? Do you mean to kill me as you killed that Egyptian yesterday?'

Then Moses realized that his deed was known, and he fled from Egypt southwards to Ethiopia—only just in time, for Pharaoh had already sent soldiers to slay him.

In time all this was forgotten, for further troubles fell upon Egypt, and Pharaoh was smitten with the horrible disease of leprosy and died some years later, to be succeeded by his son.

But meanwhile, after doing mighty deeds in Ethiopia, Moses went to dwell in the land of the Midianites to the west of the Gulf of Aqaba, where lived the descendants of Abraham's son Midian.

Here he tended the sheep of Jethro and married his daughter Zipporah, and dwelt quietly for many years.

Meanwhile in Egypt the new Pharaoh was oppressing the Israelites more and more as they grew more and more numerous —and there was no pretence any longer but that they were deadly enemies each striving for the rule of Egypt.

But it was not Jahveh's will that the Israelites should hold Egypt or remain there. For Palestine was their Promised Land and thither Jahveh decreed that they should return and settle and become the Chosen People—the only nation in the ancient world to worship one God.

And so when Moses was eighty years old Jahveh sent a Messenger to him as he tended the flocks on Mount Horeb.

This time the Messenger appeared to Moses in the form of fire. For on a sudden Moses saw before him an acacia bush, the thorn tree of the desert, burning with fire, and not consumed nor even charred by the flames.

The Egyptians in the Red Sea. (*See page 100*)

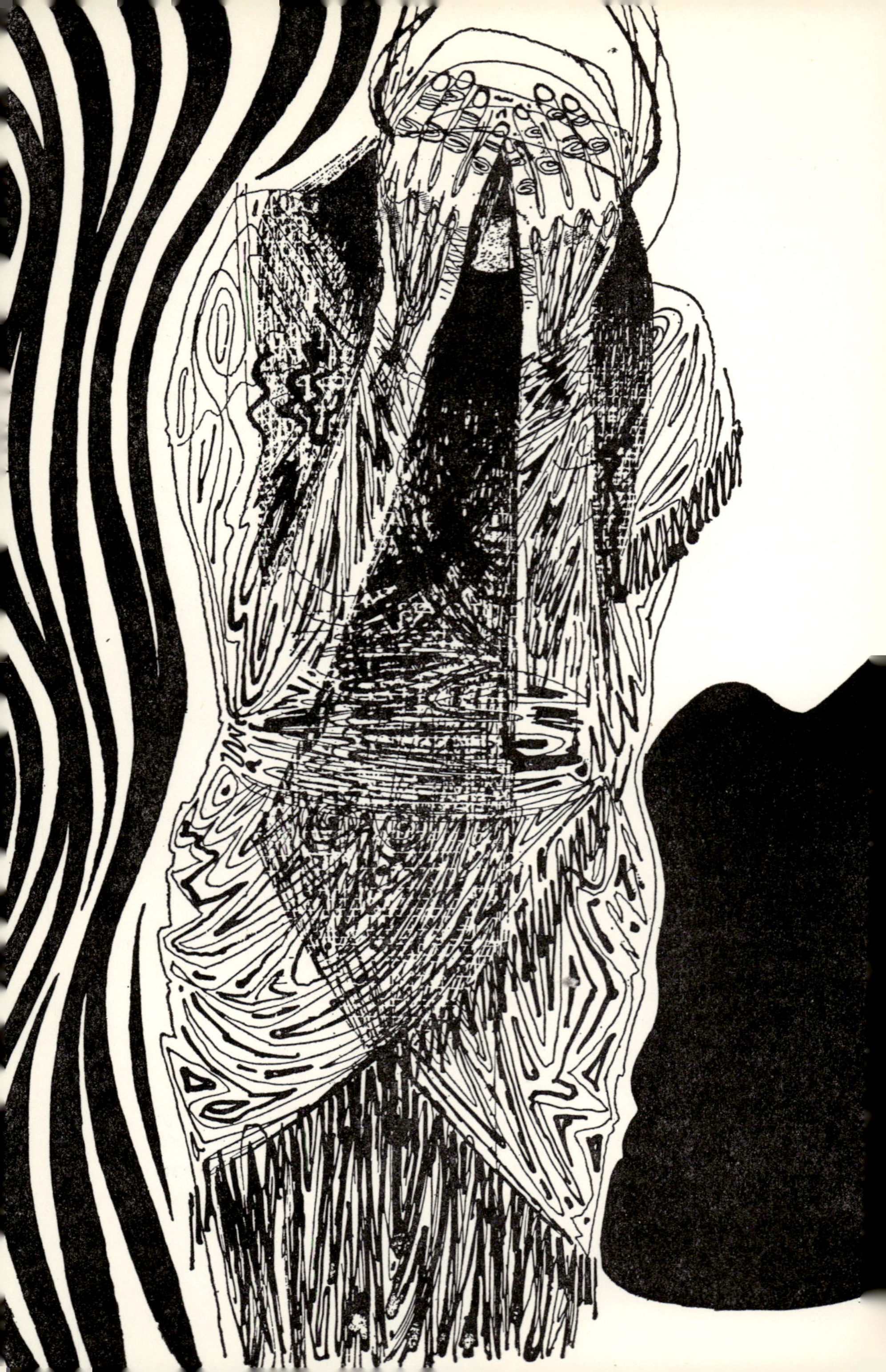

When he drew near to gaze upon this marvel, the Messenger spoke out of the burning bush, saying:

'Moses! Moses!'

And Moses answered: 'Here am I!'

Then the voice from the burning bush said: 'Do not come any nearer, but take off your shoes—for the place on which you stand is holy ground.'

When Moses had done as he was bidden the Messenger spoke again, saying: 'I speak with the voice of Jahveh, the God of Abraham, the God of Isaac, the God of Jacob. I have seen the sufferings of my people, the Children of Israel, in the land of Egypt, and I have heard their cry for help, and I know all their sorrows. Therefore I have sent my Messenger to bid you lead them out of the power of the Egyptians and to bring them out of the land where they now dwell, and into the Promised Land, the land of the Canaanites and others—a good land and a large one, a land flowing with milk and honey. Therefore go now to Pharaoh, and bring my people, the Children of Israel, out of Egypt.'

But Moses cried: 'Who am I that I should go to Pharaoh and take away the Children of Israel out of his land? And how shall my people know that I have indeed been sent to lead them?'

Then the voice answered out of the burning bush: 'Jahveh, the one God, shall be with you, and you shall tell the Children of Israel that it is indeed the God of Abraham and Isaac and Jacob who has sent you to lead them. As for Pharaoh, he will not readily let you go—no, not unless you show that you are stronger than he. Therefore Jahveh shall stretch out his hand and smite Egypt with terrible things and do many wonders until at last Pharaoh lets you go. Yes, your people shall march forth in triumph, having robbed the Egyptians of as much gold and jewellery as they can carry.'

Moses was still frightened by the greatness of his task, and said:

'What, however, if the people do not trust or listen to my words? Suppose they refuse to believe that Jahveh has spoken to me?'

The Messenger spoke out of the burning bush, saying: 'Moses! Moses!'

'What do you carry in your hand?' asked the voice from the burning bush.

'A rod,' answered Moses.

'Throw it on the ground!' came the command. And as he did so the rod turned into a snake and Moses sprang back in fear.

'Put out your hand and take it by the tail,' said the voice.

Though much afraid, Moses did so. At once the snake turned back into the rod in his hand—the same rod which he had always carried and which his father-in-law had given to him saying that it had been cut by Adam in the Garden of Eden.

'If they do not believe the sign of the rod', said the voice of Jahveh's Messenger, 'you may show them another sign. Put your hand into the front of your robe.'

Moses did so, and when he drew it out it was white with leprosy.

'Put it back into your robe', said the voice, 'and it will become whole, and free from the disease of which the late Pharaoh died and which the Egyptians accuse the Children of Israel of bringing to their land. And if the people do not believe either of these signs, nor hearken to your words, take water from the Nile and pour it upon the dry land—and it shall turn into blood.'

Moses still hesitated and looked for excuses, saying: 'I am not a man of easy or persuasive words. I am slow of speech and not of a ready tongue.'

'Question no more, but obey the commands of Jahveh!' cried the voice of the Messenger out of the fire in the burning bush. 'As you return to Goshen your brother Aaron shall meet you. Let him be ever at your side, for he shall be your spokesman if words fail you. But take your rod in your hand and go!'

Then the fire faded and passed away as the Messenger returned whence he came, and the bush stood unharmed on the hillside without so much as a single leaf or blossom shrivelled.

THE TEN PLAGUES

AFTER Jahveh's Messenger had spoken to him out of the burning bush, Moses bade farewell to Jethro, his father-in-law, and set out for Egypt. As he came down the north-western slopes of Mount Horeb into the wilderness of Sinai he met his brother Aaron, whom a Messenger of Jahveh had sent to seek him.

Moses told him of the commands laid upon him by Jahveh, and of the signs which he had been given power to show to the Children of Israel, and together they journeyed in haste to Goshen.

Here they summoned a gathering of the elders of Israel, and Aaron made a great speech to them telling of all that Moses had been bidden to do. And after this Moses showed the signs of the rod which turned into a snake, and his hand which became that of a leper, and of the Nile water that turned to blood.

All these things convinced the elders and the people of Israel that Moses had truly been sent by Jahveh to lead them out of Egypt and into the Promised Land of Canaan, and they made him their leader and vowed to follow him and to do all that he commanded.

Then Moses and Aaron took their rods in their hands and went up to Pharaoh's palace at Heliopolis and into Pharaoh's presence, and said:

'Jahveh, the great God of Israel, has laid his command upon us and upon you that you let all the Children of Israel and all their people journey three days into the wilderness to hold a great feast in his honour.'

But Pharaoh cried: 'Who is this Jahveh of whom you speak? I do not know him, and he is no god of mine or of Egypt. Why should I obey these commands which you say are his? Jahveh means nothing to me—and I will not let Israel go.'

'Jahveh has appeared to us on his holy mount of Horeb,' said Aaron. 'And we beg you to let us go three days into the wilderness to sacrifice and hold a feast in his honour, lest he punish us with illness or death for our disobedience.'

'The people of Israel shall indeed be punished,' cried Pharaoh, 'and they may blame you alone for daring to keep them from their work! Go back to Goshen and do your own share in it!'

Then he turned to the commander of the overseers and taskmasters, whose duty was to make sure that the Israelites did their full amount of work each day, and said:

'These rebellious slaves in Goshen must be taught a lesson. Therefore do not give them straw any longer for making the bricks with which they are building my city of Ramses. Let them hunt for and gather the straw for themselves. But I will allow no falling off in the number of bricks which they make: see to it that there is not one less than when you supplied the straw. Make them work! They are becoming idle, if they think they have time to go and sacrifice to their god in the wilderness—so give them more labour rather than less, and pay no attention to their foolish words.'

Then the overseers and taskmasters went among the Israelites proclaiming the commands of Pharaoh; and the people were scattered through the land gathering the stubble from the fields to use for straw.

Whenever the number of bricks made in a day was less than before, the Israelite foremen in command of each shift were taken and beaten by the Egyptian overseers, who demanded: 'Why have you failed to do a full day's work? The same number of bricks is expected each day—yesterday and today and tomorrow.'

Then the foremen from among the Israelites came in a body to Pharaoh and complained to him, saying:

'Why are you treating your labourers like this? We have no straw given to us, but the overseers insist that we make as many bricks as ever—and if we fail to do so we are beaten, although it is not our fault.'

But Pharaoh replied: 'You are idle and lazy—and then you ask for time off to go and sacrifice to Jahveh. Get back to your work, and be sure that no straw will be given to you, but as many bricks will be expected of you as ever.'

Then the foremen realized that they were in for much trouble and hardship, and they turned against Moses and Aaron and cursed them, saying:

'This is all your fault—and may Jahveh punish you for it! Look at the evil you have brought on us, and the excuse you have given Pharaoh and his servants to persecute and kill us!'

This troubled Moses greatly, and he prayed to Jahveh, saying: 'Is this what you promised me? I have obeyed the words of your Messenger, and the only result is that the people of Israel suffer still further misery, and there is no sign of them being delivered out of bondage in the land of Egypt.'

Again Jahveh's message came to Moses to strengthen him, and once more he and Aaron repeated Jahveh's promise to the people of Israel to bring them out of Egypt in triumph and give them the land of Canaan to be their home.

But they would not listen or believe any more, on account of all that they were suffering from the Egyptian overseers and taskmasters.

Then Jahveh spoke again to Moses, telling him how he would harden Pharaoh's heart against Israel so that he would not let the people go until the Egyptians had suffered many and terrible things. And, following all that Jahveh had commanded, Moses and Aaron took their rods in their hands and presented themselves once more before Pharaoh.

And when they stood in his presence they cried: 'Pharaoh! Pharaoh! Pharaoh! Let the people of Israel go—for if you do not Jahveh our God will smite you and all Egypt with terrible plagues, and bring sorrow and desolation upon you and all the people of Egypt.'

Then Pharaoh laughed and said: 'What power have you or your false god? If you have any show me a sign!'

At once Aaron cast his rod onto the ground and it turned into a snake. But Pharaoh merely turned to his own magicians and they, by their magic, did likewise, casting down their rods and turning them into serpents until the floor of Pharaoh's hall was one hissing mass.

But Aaron waved his arms, and cried upon Jahveh, and at once the snake which had been his rod turned and swallowed all the Egyptian snakes one after another. Then it became a rod once more, and Aaron picked it up and leant upon it as he waited for Pharaoh's answer.

Pharaoh would give no answer that day, however. But as soon as Moses and Aaron had gone he sent orders to his officers to have their troops ready to guard the frontiers of Goshen lest the Israelites should try to march out into the wilderness.

Moses had his orders from Jahveh also and next day he went down to the landing-place on the Nile near which he had been found as a baby.

Presently Pharaoh and his court came down to the riverside and made ready to enter the royal boat for a trip on the Nile.

But Moses stepped forward and cried: 'Pharaoh! Pharaoh! Pharaoh! Will you let my people go?'

'I will not let them go!' answered Pharaoh angrily.

'Then behold the wrath of Jahveh and his strength!' cried Moses, and struck the water of the Nile with his rod. And at once all the water of the river was turned to blood, and the fish died, and the river stank from their dead bodies, and the Egyptians could not drink the Nile water for seven days, but were forced to dig wells into which the water could filter through the sand.

But the Israelites drank easily, for the night before the Nile was turned to blood they had filled all their pots and jars with fresh water.

The magicians of Egypt, however, were also able to turn

water into blood, and Pharaoh was even more enraged against Moses and less inclined to let the Children of Israel go.

Then Moses and Aaron came again into his presence, and when he refused to let the people go Aaron stretched out his rod, and at once out of the Nile and out of the pools and marshes in the Delta came great hosts of frogs. There were frogs everywhere: in the houses, in the bedrooms, in the beds, in the ovens and the cooking pots, in Pharaoh's palace and in the houses of all the Egyptians—but not in or near the dwellings of any of the Children of Israel.

Very soon Pharaoh sent for Moses and Aaron and said: 'Pray to your god Jahveh to take away the frogs from me and my subjects, and I will let your people go to make their sacrifice in the wilderness.'

'Tomorrow', said Moses, 'there shall be frogs only in the Nile, for those everywhere else shall die, and your people can sweep them up and burn them.'

And all happened as he said, and the stench of the burning frogs filled all Egypt. But when the frogs had gone Pharaoh hardened his heart and would not let the Israelites go.

So Aaron stretched out his rod once more, and the dust of Egypt turned into lice which bit both man and beast among the Egyptians, but did not trouble the Israelites.

Now Pharaoh's magicians had been able to produce frogs by their magic, but lice were beyond them, and they said: 'This is the doing of a god—our magic can reach no further.'

Pharaoh's heart was still hardened, however, and he would not let the Israelites go, in spite of the lice.

But Moses came before him again as he was going down to the royal boat and said: 'Hear the words of Jahveh: "Let my people go or else I will send swarms of flies upon you, and upon your servants, and upon your people, and into your palace; and the houses of the Egyptians shall be full of swarms of flies, and flies shall crawl upon the ground. But no flies shall come to the land of Goshen where my people dwell—and this will prove to Pharaoh that I am the one God above all other gods."'

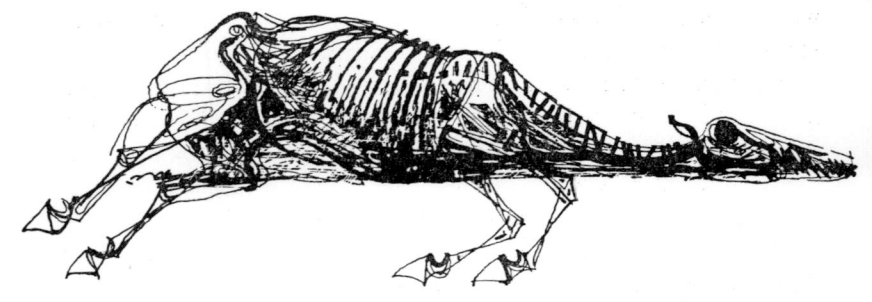

All the beasts sickened with the cattle plague

When Pharaoh again would not let the people of Israel go the swarms of flies settled all over the land of Egypt, and he sent in haste for Moses, saying:

'You and all your people may sacrifice to your god—but in Goshen, and not in the wilderness.'

'We cannot sacrifice there,' answered Moses, 'for the Egyptians will stone us when they see us slaying the beasts which they hold sacred.'

'Then go one day's journey into the desert of Sinai,' said Pharaoh, 'and pray to your god that he may deliver Egypt from this plague of flies.'

But when the flies had ceased to trouble him Pharaoh went back on his word again, and Moses came before him and laid a curse on all the cattle in Egypt, and the camels and horses and donkeys and oxen and sheep. Soon they all sickened with the murrain, or cattle plague, and a great many of them died; but not one beast belonging to the Israelites suffered at all.

When Pharaoh learned that only the Egyptians' beasts were afflicted he grew more and more angry with the Children of Israel, and, far from letting them go, urged the overseers to lay still heavier tasks on them and beat them even to death if they tried to shirk.

Soon, however, Moses and Aaron came before him again, and when he refused to let the people of Israel go they cast handfuls of ashes into the air, and the dust spread through Egypt, and wherever one speck of it landed on man or beast it caused a painful boil to break out.

When Pharaoh bade his magicians bring boils and blains upon Moses and Aaron they could not even stand up before them since their very feet were covered with boils.

'Since you will not let my people go, hear how next Jahveh will curse you!' cried Moses. 'He will smite you and yours from heaven, and few shall escape unhurt. But no ill shall befall any among the people of Israel.'

Moses and Aaron returned to Goshen and instructed the Israelites to bring all their livestock under cover, and themselves take shelter in houses and caves.

As soon as they were all safe the clouds rolled up over Egypt, and such a shower of hail fell as had never been known before—nor has any such shower fallen since.

The thunder roared and the hail beat down, and many were killed or wounded by the jagged lumps of ice, while the crops were beaten flat and the fruit was stripped from the trees.

But in Goshen hardly any hail fell; little damage was done, and neither man nor beast suffered any harm.

This time Pharaoh was really frightened. He sent in haste for Moses and said to him:

'Osar-seph, now I know that Jahveh your god is stronger than Amen-Ra, and Horus and Isis, and all the gods of Egypt. I have sinned against Jahveh, and I and all my people are in the wrong. Therefore pray to Jahveh that there may be no more thunder and hail over Egypt, and I will let you go and keep you in bondage no longer.'

Then Moses replied: 'As soon as I have gone out of this city, I will raise my arms in prayer to Jahveh, and the thunder shall cease, and there shall be no more hail.'

Soon the storm ceased and the clouds rolled away, leaving Egypt in a sorry state, for the barley and the flax were all destroyed since they were nearly ripe; but the rest of the corn, such as wheat and rye, escaped since it was barely above the ground.

The Israelites rejoiced, thinking that now at last they would be free. But when the sky was blue again and the undamaged corn began to push through the earth, Pharaoh forgot his fear and would not let them go.

So Moses and Aaron came before him yet again and said: 'Pharaoh! Pharaoh! Pharaoh! Hear the words of Jahveh: "How long will you refuse to humble yourself before me? Let my people go so that they can serve me—or else tomorrow I will bring a plague of locusts to cover the earth and eat all that the hail has left, both crops and grass and the green leaves on the trees."'

Then Pharaoh's counsellors cried: 'O Pharaoh—life, health, strength be to you, let these people go, for their magic is destroying Egypt!'

And Pharaoh said to Moses: 'I will let you go into the wilderness to serve Jahveh. But first, tell me who of your number must take part in these rites?'

'We will go with our young and our old, our sons and our daughters, our flocks and our herds,' answered Moses.

'That I will not allow!' cried Pharaoh. 'You and all the grown men of the Israelites may go to serve Jahveh—for that is what you wish. But the women and the children, the flocks and the herds, shall stay behind as hostages.'

Moses and Aaron tried to argue, but at a sign from Pharaoh they were seized and driven out of the palace.

So Moses waved his rod over the land of Egypt and called down a plague of locusts. At first a strong wind blew from out of the east, and in the morning it brought the locusts from beyond the Red Sea, and they settled on all the east coast of Egypt in clouds and began to eat every green thing that the hail had left.

Then Pharaoh sent for Moses and Aaron in a hurry and said: 'I have done wrong, and sinned against both you and your god. I beg you to forgive me, and pray to Jahveh to forgive me also—and I will not offend again.'

So Moses lifted up his rod and waved it once more. And the wind changed and blew steadily from the west, carrying all the locusts—alive or dead—into the Red Sea, until there was not one left on the Egyptian coast.

But even now Pharaoh would not take warning and let the Israelites go. So Moses stretched out his rod once more, and darkness fell over all the land of Egypt—a darkness so dense that it could almost be felt. And this thick darkness lasted for three days and nights.

In the end Pharaoh was forced to send for Moses, and when the darkness was ended he said:

'Now you may go to serve Jahveh—all of you, man, woman and child. Only you must leave your flocks and herds behind.'

'We must take them all with us,' lied Moses boldly, 'for we cannot tell which of them Jahveh will choose to be sacrificed to him.'

'Go!' commanded Pharaoh. 'This is my final decree, and I shall not change it. Moreover do not come into my presence ever again, for if I see you again, then you die.'

'You have spoken the truth,' said Moses grimly, 'for we shall not meet again.'

Then Moses went out from Pharaoh's presence for the last time. But soon he was speaking not to Pharaoh but to all the people of Egypt, crying:

'If Pharaoh does not let the people of Israel go into the wilderness, man, woman and child, with all their flocks and herds, to sacrifice to Jahveh, then Jahveh will smite Egypt at the hour of midnight and slay all the first-born; from the first-born of Pharaoh himself to the first-born of his lowest servant; and the first-born of the beasts shall perish also. There shall be a great cry of sorrow ringing through the land of Egypt tomorrow—such a cry as has never been heard before nor will be again.'

Moses then gathered the Israelites together and said to them: 'When Jahveh smites the Egyptians, not one of the Children of Israel shall suffer. And tomorrow we go. But now take each of you a lamb—one lamb for each household—a male lamb, without blemish. Kill it and splash its blood on either doorpost and the upper lintel of your houses, for Jahveh shall send his Messenger of Death through Egypt tonight to smite the first-born—but he will enter no house that is marked with the blood of a lamb. And this shall be celebrated by us and by our descendants in memory of this night: it shall be called the Feast of the Passover—for the Angel of Death shall pass over the houses of the Children of Israel and spare all who dwell in them.

'When you have slain the lamb and splashed its blood on the door frame, you may roast and eat its meat. With it take unleavened bread and fresh herbs; and eat your meal ready dressed for your journey. The bread shall be unleavened, for there is no time to add the yeast and wait for it to rise; the herbs shall be fresh, for there is no time to dry them; and the lamb's meat shall be roast, since that is the quickest way of cooking it.

'And when the sun rises, be ready to march: man, woman and child of you, with your flocks and herds and all that you can carry of your possessions. Moreover you should borrow jewels and silver and gold from the Egyptians; of course you will not give these treasures back, but the Egyptians will not realize this, since they think that we are only going into the wilderness for three days to sacrifice to Jahveh. But in fact we set out at sunrise for the Promised Land!'

THE DOWNFALL OF PHARAOH

THAT night none of the Children of Israel slept. In haste they slew their lambs, splashed the blood on the doorposts and lintels, and set the meat to roast. While it was cooking they looked to their sandals and buckled them on to their feet, put on their coats and fastened their belts.

At midnight the Messenger of Jahveh, Azrael the Angel of Death, passed over the land of Egypt and slew the first-born of all who dwelt there, from the eldest son of Pharaoh to the eldest child of the captive in his dungeon, and the first-born of the cattle also. But over every house marked with the three splashes of blood Azrael passed without touching any of the inmates with his sword—and not one of the Israelites nor of their cattle died that night.

Azrael passed. And there rose a whisper through all the land of Egypt that grew to a murmur and then to a cry—such a cry of woe as has never been heard before or since. All the people of Egypt wept and lamented at the cruel death of their children.

Then they turned upon the Israelites and drove them out. They dared not harm them, fearing that the terrible power which had murdered their children should kill them also. But they saw to it that with the coming of day every man, woman and child of Israel, with all their flocks and herds and baggage animals, were on their way from Goshen, north-east towards Pi-Aten or Succoth on the way to the deserts beyond the Bitter Lakes at the north of that branch of the Red Sea into which the Suez Canal now leads.

As they went the Israelites, remembering the words of Moses, helped themselves to as much gold and jewels and fine garments as they could carry. And the Egyptians dared not refuse any of these 'loans'—which they knew as well as the Israelites would never be returned.

That evening the hosts of Israel camped at Succoth—six hundred thousand of them, besides women and children and camp followers. They made cakes from the dough which they carried with them—for there was no time to leaven it and bake bread, and they were driven out so quickly that they could take no other provisions.

However, they took with them the coffin which held Joseph's mummified body, so keeping the promise which had been made to him on his deathbed of burying him in the land of Canaan where lay the bones of Abraham and Isaac and Jacob.

The next day they continued on their journey, Jahveh sending a pillar of cloud by day and a pillar of fire by night to lead them in the way they should go. And this way was not by the shortest route across the desert by the sea coast; for there dwelt the Philistines against whom the Israelites were not yet strong enough to fight. Instead their route ran across the Bitter Lakes into the Desert of Etham, down the coast of Sinai, across to Midian and so up the Gulf of Aqaba.

That night they rested at Etham on the edge of the desert, a day's journey from the Bitter Lakes, and by the following evening had reached the shore, for in those days the Bitter Lakes were part of the Gulf of Suez at the very north of the Red Sea.

Meanwhile the news was brought to Pharaoh that the Israelites were wandering in the wilderness down the wrong side of the Red Sea, which was cutting them off from Sinai and the way to Palestine.

Then Pharaoh and his counsellors said among themselves: 'Why have we let these people go? We should have kept them to be our slaves.'

The people of Egypt were also crying out that the Israelites should be destroyed or enslaved on account of the deaths of the first-born; and at last Pharaoh decided to pursue them.

So he took six hundred of his fastest chariots, and a regiment

The priests blew their trumpets. (*See page 119*)

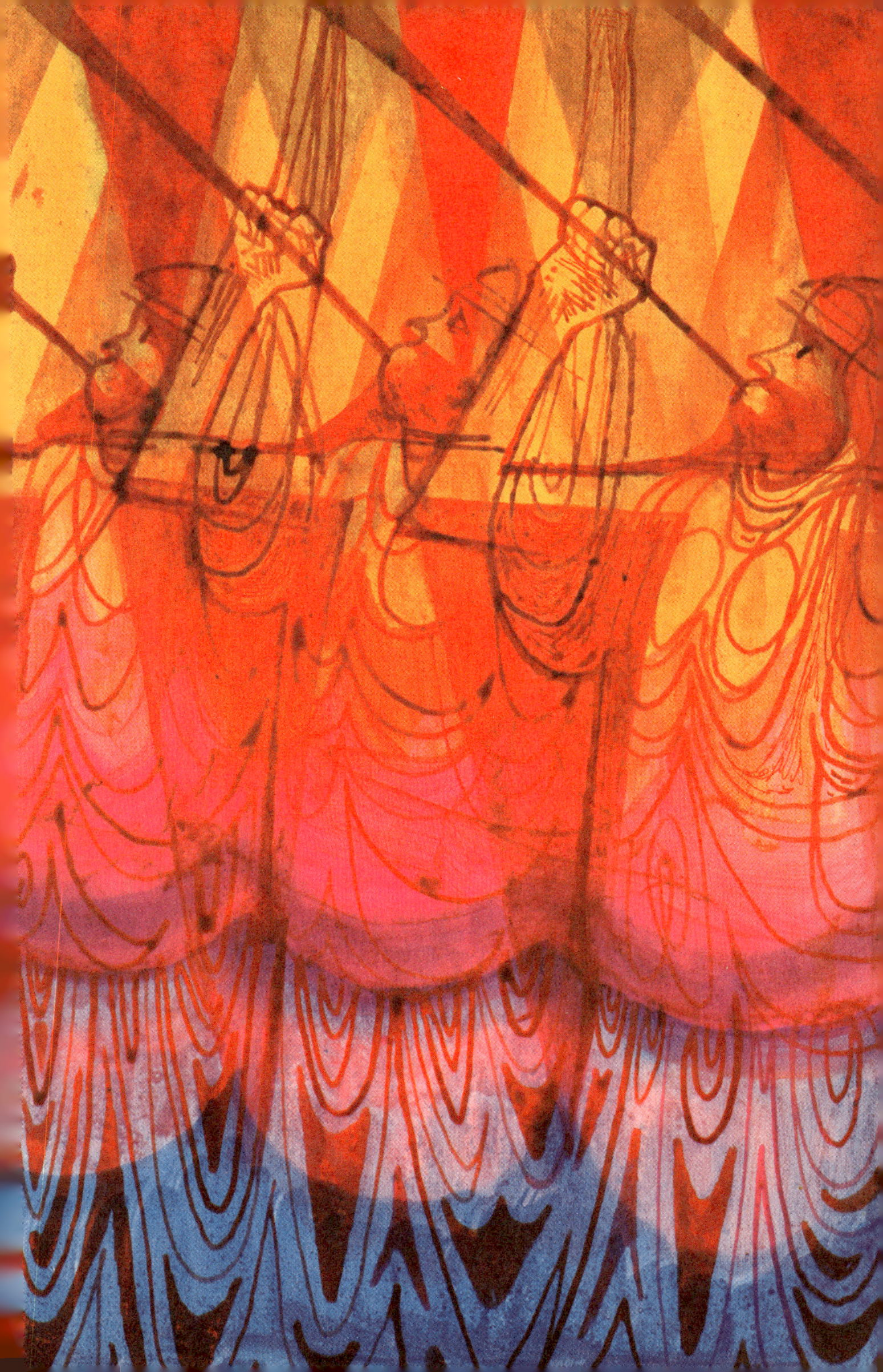

of horse, and set out by a short way through the hills by a pass that lies between Heliopolis and Ramses.

The Egyptian army came into view as the sun was setting on the third day of the Israelites' flight. And when they saw it they were filled with panic, and thronged round Moses, crying:

'Were there no graves for us in Egypt that you have brought us out to perish in the wilderness? Why have you betrayed us like this? Did we not tell you to let us live peacefully in Egypt—where it would have been better to serve the Egyptians than to die here?'

'Do not be afraid,' answered Moses, 'but trust in Jahveh, who will fight for you. As for these Egyptians, you are looking upon them for the last time.'

Scarcely had he spoken when the Messenger of Jahveh, who had appeared to them as the pillar of cloud and fire, moved from in front of them and settled on the desert behind, forming a smoke screen between them and Pharaoh's army. To the Egyptians it seemed that dark night had fallen between them and their enemies; but to the Israelites the cloud shone more brightly than the full moon and lit up all their camp, making a silver pathway of light across the strip of sea that separated them from the Desert of Etham beyond the gulf.

Then Moses stood upon the shore and raised his hands in prayer. Soon a great wind began to blow from the north; stronger and stronger it blew until the waters of the gulf drew back before it and made a huge bank of water, leaving the sand clear and dry behind it.

The wall of water was like a dam holding back the sea, and Moses pointed to the dry land that had been the sea-bed and cried:

'See the pathway to the Promised Land that Jahveh has made for you! Pass over by it quickly so that all may be on the farther shore before the Egyptians come after us with the dawning.'

And the Children of Israel went down the gentle slope of sand and passed across the sea on the dry land which had been beneath the waves. All night their columns passed across the sea-bed, and when the sun rose the last of them were just drawing near the coast of Etham.

With the dawn the pillar of cloud disappeared from before the Egyptians, and Pharaoh saw how the great wind was driving the sea back in a sloping wall of water to leave a dry path for the Israelites to cross.

'There go our escaping slaves!' he cried. 'Where Israelites can tread we can follow! After them and slay until none be left except such captives as we need for slaves!'

So the chariots and the horsemen poured down the bank and out onto the sea bottom where the Israelites had passed. But they went more slowly, since the wheels of their chariots sank in the soft sand, and their horses' hooves were clogged by it as if they were crossing a marsh.

By the time the last Israelite was above the water line on the eastern shore all the Egyptian horsemen and chariots were on the sea-bed, rapidly overtaking them.

Then Moses turned back towards Egypt, raised his hands once more, and cried aloud to Jahveh to destroy the Egyptians and rescue his people from them.

As he spoke the great wind fell suddenly and moaned away into silence. And as it died the waters of the Red Sea slid back into their place and swept once more up to the head of the Gulf of Suez.

The Egyptians turned to fly from before the sliding wall of water, but there was no time. In a moment it had covered and swept away all the horsemen and the chariots; and of all the army that had come out to capture and slay the Children of Israel, not one that had gone down onto the sea-bed remained alive.

And seeing how great a miracle Jahveh had performed to save them, the Children of Israel fell down and worshipped him. And Moses made a song of triumph for them to sing, praising Jahveh and telling how he had utterly destroyed their enemies the Egyptians beneath the waters of the Red Sea.

Also Miriam the prophetess, sister of Moses and Aaron, led the women in a victory dance, singing as they waved and struck their timbrels or tambourines, and rejoicing on their escape out of the land of Egypt.

THROUGH THE WILDERNESS

The Israelites had escaped from Egypt and were out of reach of Pharaoh's armies; but they had not by any means come to the Promised Land, and many troubles still lay in front of them before they would cross the River Jordan and come to the holy place where Jerusalem was to be built.

Directly after they had crossed the north-western tip of the Red Sea they set out towards the south, keeping a little distance inland since many Egyptian ships sailed down the Gulf of Suez to ports on the Red Sea coast and beyond.

After three days in the wilderness of Shur they came to a well of water and rejoiced, for all that they had carried with them was used up, and they were beginning to suffer from thirst.

But when they tasted the water they found it was bitter and undrinkable. At once they began to murmur and complain to Moses, saying: 'What can we drink? This great well of water is useless.'

Moses had, however, been told by Jahveh what to do. He found a special tree which, when cut down and dipped into the well, made the water wholesome and drinkable.

Three days' march beyond Marah, the Well of Bitterness, they came safely to Elim where there were no less than twelve wells, all of pure water. And here they camped to rest and prepare themselves for the journey across the desert and mountains of Sinai.

But when they set out again on their way through the Desert of Sinai, they soon began to murmur and complain once more at the hardness and discomfort, and at the shortage of food and water.

'If only we had died quickly and easily in Egypt!' they

lamented. 'There at least we had as much good bread and meat as we wanted. But now you have brought us into this desert, so that we shall all die of hunger and thirst.'

Moses withdrew into his tent and prayed to Jahveh. And during the night a Messenger came to him and told him how Jahveh would feed his people for however long they were in the wilderness, and until they came to the border of the Promised Land.

Next morning he and Aaron called all the people together, and Moses spoke to them, saying: 'Bow down before the might and mercy of Jahveh, for he has heard your complaints and promised that every morning you shall eat all the bread you need, and every evening all the meat for as long as you are in the wilderness between here and Canaan.

'Every evening bevies of quails will come flying low over your camps, and you may catch them in nets until you have as many as you need. And every morning if you go out into the desert you will find the ground strewn with small round objects no bigger than hailstones: gather these and you may make of them a bread that tastes of honey and wafers.'

That night the quails came down, bevy after bevy, and the Israelites caught them in their nets until they had enough for all the camp to eat their fill of roast meat. And next morning they went out and found the strange little pellets scattered under the tamarisk bushes, and gathered them up in basketsful. And, never having seen them before, they asked in the speech of Israel '*Man na? Man na?*', meaning 'What is it? What is it?' But as it had no name they called it manna from that day on.

The manna was so good that the greedy Israelites would have collected far more than they needed. But Moses stopped this, saying:

'Collect only what you need for the day. For any that you keep will not last.'

Many, however, disobeyed him. But next morning when they came to eat it they found only a stinking mass of maggots. Also they soon discovered that they must get up early to collect the manna, for if the sun shone on it it melted away.

Now the Israelites were able to continue on their journey with no further anxiety about food. But sometimes they were short of water, and one of the worst occasions was when they had reached Horeb, the earliest of the great peaks of the Sinai range.

As soon as they were in trouble the Israelites at once forgot how Jahveh had helped them and came whining and clamouring to Moses, crying:

'Give us water so that we may drink! Why have you brought us out of Egypt to die of thirst in this terrible place—us, and our children and our flocks and herds?'

Then, in despair, Moses cried to Jahveh, saying: 'What shall I do with this people? As soon as anything goes wrong they are ready to stone me!'

But Jahveh was patient with the people, and he showed Moses what to do. And Moses went to a great rock that stuck out at the foot of Horeb and struck it with his rod—and at once water gushed out and all were able to drink.

Not long after this the Israelites came in for their first bit of fighting when Amalek, the king of that country, and his Amalekites came against them.

But Moses chose the best warrior among the Israelites, Joshua the son of Nun, who was a descendant of Joseph's younger son Ephraim, to command the fighting men, and sent them out against the Amalekites.

Moses meanwhile climbed up a hill to watch the battle, and with him went Aaron and his brother-in-law Hur, Miriam's husband. So long as Moses held up his arms, Israel showed signs of winning; but when he lowered them, Amalek seemed likely to be the victor. But Moses was old, and his arms were heavy, and he could not hold them up for long. So Aaron and Hur sat him down on the big stone and stood one on either side of him, holding up his arms. And there they stood until the sun went down; and when darkness came the Amalekites turned and fled, leaving Joshua and the Israelites masters of the field of battle.

By the time they came at last to the very foot of Mount Sinai the Israelites had been three months on their way from Egypt.

And here they camped for a much longer stay, since Jahveh had instructed Moses that this should be so, and that here the Law and the Promise were to be given to them, and they would become Jahveh's Chosen People, the Nation of Israel—a kingdom of priests and a holy nation.

'Jahveh has commanded me to go up to the top of Mount Sinai,' Moses told Aaron and the people. 'There he will draw near to me in a great black cloud, with lightnings and thunder, and speak to me as he or his Messenger spoke to me once before out of the burning bush. While I am gone let no one stir a single step up the mountain, for any who does shall die. But from here you will see the great cloud and hear the voice of Jahveh so that your faith may grow strong, and you may never again doubt that there is but one God, by whose will you have come safely out of Egypt and will go safely into the Promised Land of Canaan; and by whose decree you are the Chosen People among whom shall be accomplished the great purpose of God.

'Now for three days you must purify yourselves and sacrifice to Jahveh and pray to him. Then I shall go up on to Sinai to receive the Law; and you must humble yourselves and bow down in worship in the very presence of Jahveh.'

All happened as Moses had said. And on the morning of the third day there were thunders and lightnings, and a thick cloud gathered over the mountain, and a sound like a very shrill and loud trumpet.

The people were greatly scared by all this. But Moses led them out of the camp to the foot of Mount Sinai; and as they looked up the rocky path to the summit it seemed as if the whole mountain was on fire; and it shook as if there were an earthquake.

Then Jahveh spoke out of the dark cloud, and his words were the Ten Commandments that all peoples in all ages must obey. But his voice sounded so terrible to the Israelites that they drew back in fear from the foot of the mountain and cried to Moses:

'Tell us what Jahveh says, but do not make us hearken to his voice, or we shall die of fear.'

'Do not be afraid,' said Moses. 'Jahveh has spoken only to prove your worth, that you may obey his words, and fear his anger if you disobey or fall into sin. Keep away now from the mountain, and I will go up and learn the further will of Jahveh. When I return I will tell you all that Jahveh has said, so that it can be written down on rolls and preserved for you and your descendants to read and obey. But the great commandments Jahveh himself will write upon tablets of stone, and these I will bring down with me when I return.'

Then Moses went up Mount Sinai until he disappeared from sight in the dark cloud that rested on its summit. And there he remained for many days and nights, learning not only the Ten Commandments that are for all mankind for ever, but also the many rules of life and conduct, of religious observance and sacrifice, and of the future doings of the Children of Israel. Just as a father, before he leaves this world, makes known his last will and testament to his children, so Jahveh through the mind and pen of Moses made his known to the people of Israel; and it was written down in the first books of the Bible, and became their rules of life—until the new testament was made for all mankind in the life and teaching of Christ.

When his mind was stored with all that he must teach the people of Israel, Moses came slowly down the mountain carrying with him the two stone tablets on which Jahveh had inscribed the Ten Commandments.

But meanwhile the Israelites had grown tired of waiting for Moses. Their shallow minds forgot the wonders they had seen and the very voice of Jahveh which they had heard, and the knowledge which had been given to them alone, making them the Chosen People, that there was but one God in all the universe. And they surged round Aaron crying:

'Make us gods to worship and to follow! This man Moses who led us out of Egypt is lost on the mountain. His teaching is too hard for us, and we want idols of gold to worship like other people.'

'Then bring me the golden earrings which your wives and

your sons and your daughters wear,' answered Aaron, 'and I will make you a god.'

So they brought the golden ornaments which they had stolen from the Egyptians, and Aaron melted them with fire and shaped the gold with an engraving tool and made a great golden calf and set it up on a pedestal.

Then he caused a stone altar to be built in front of it, and cried:

'Here is your god which brought you out of Egypt and will lead you to Canaan!' And the people all worshipped the golden calf, and rejoiced that they had a god which they could see, like the many images of bull and cow and cat and crocodile gods which they had known in Egypt.

'Tomorrow we will hold a great feast in honour of this our god!' proclaimed Aaron. And next day the people sacrificed sheep and cattle to the golden calf, and feasted and drank and made merry.

This was the day on which Moses came down the mountain. And when he had left the cloud behind him he found Joshua and a band of his followers waiting for him.

As they journeyed down Mount Sinai together they heard the sounds of many voices from the camp below them, and Joshua said:

'Listen! There is a noise of war in the camp! Maybe the Amalekites have attacked again.'

But Moses knew better, and he said: 'It is not the cheers of the victors, nor the cries of the victims in battle, but a sound of singing and revelry.'

A few moments later they came round a corner of rock and looked down upon the camp. And when Moses saw the golden calf and the people worshipping it, and men and women dancing naked before it like shameless idolators, such a wave of anger surged over him that he flung down the sacred tablets of the Law and they were shattered to pieces.

Then Moses cried to Aaron: 'What have you done? Why have you helped the people of Israel to commit this great sin?'

Aaron flung himself on his knees before Moses and said: 'Do

not be too angry with me, for you know how cruel our people are when they are bent on evil. To save my life I had to obey them when they commanded me to make them an idol to worship. I told them to bring me their golden ornaments to melt down, thinking they were too miserly to part with anything so valuable —but they brought them. I made the gold into a calf and told them to worship it, thinking they would be ashamed to do anything so ridiculous—but they fell down and adored it. I told them that they must appoint priests and priestesses to dance naked before it after the manner of those who worship Baal and Ashtoreth, thinking they would be ashamed to practise such obscenities—but you see what they are doing!'

Moses turned to the people of Israel and cried in a great voice that rang over all the camp and drowned the prayers and hymns to the golden calf:

'Who among you is upon Jahveh's side? Who believes in the one true God who has brought us out of Egypt and will give to you and your children the Promised Land—the land flowing with milk and honey—if you are but faithful to him? Let all those come to me. But those who would worship a lump of gold carved to look like one of the least of the beasts of the field—let them tremble before the vengeance of Jahveh!'

Then many gathered round Moses, notably the descendants of Levi from whom the priests of Jahveh were appointed; but most of the people still hesitated.

'Draw your swords,' commanded Moses, 'and go down through the camp. There slay without mercy all those who have cast off their garments to practise the shameless rites of the heathen.'

The Levites did as they were commanded, and the rest of the Israelites fled in terror to their tents.

Next morning at Moses' command the golden calf was ground into powder which was mixed with water and given to the people to drink.

Then Moses said: 'You have sinned a great sin, and I must return onto the mountain to see if Jahveh will forgive you. For your life's sake do not fall into any more temptation while I am away.'

Moses returned to the top of Sinai, where he remained for forty days and nights, and then returned carrying fresh tablets of stone on which the Ten Commandments were inscribed. But this time they were not written by Jahveh but by Moses at his dictation.

But Moses seemed to shine with light when he came down the mountain, and none of the Israelites doubted any more but that he had indeed spoken with Jahveh and been sent to lead them into the Promised Land.

Yet, for their sin in worshipping the golden calf, Moses was forced to tell them that Jahveh would no longer lead them through the wilderness, though he would send one of his Messengers to do so. And also that they would not come quickly or easily to the land flowing with milk and honey, but only after many years of wandering.

So they continued on their way, hither and thither in the deserts and the mountains of the Sinai pensinula, for many years. And though they drew slowly nearer to the Promised Land, they never seemed able to reach it—for in spite of all the wonders which Jahveh had shown them, and all the teachings of Moses, they kept straying from their obedience to his laws and suffering punishment and further delays in their journey.

On one occasion an Israelite was caught gathering sticks on the Sabbath day, and was stoned to death by the people, as Moses commanded.

On another, three of the leading Israelites tried to seize power, headed by a certain Korah, a Levite, who led a rebellion against Moses, accusing him of making himself a dictator when all should be equal.

They persuaded many to follow them, but all these deserted the rebels when Moses threatened them with the vengeance of Jahveh. And sure enough Korah and his two friends were swallowed up by the earth with all their wives and children, and went down living into the pit.

'It is not wise to rebel against those whom Jahveh has chosen to lead you,' said Moses to the Israelites. 'And to prove who is to be your high priest, and his children after him, choose one man from each tribe and let him set up his rod in the earth before the tent in which the tablets of the Law are kept.'

They did as Moses commanded; and next morning the rod of Aaron, chief priest of the tribe of Levi, had taken root and was burgeoning and bringing forth buds which soon blossomed and yielded almonds. But the other eleven rods remained no more than bare, dead sticks.

After this no one dared doubt that the Levites were the priestly tribe and Aaron and his descendants were to be the high priests of Israel.

Again, when towards the end of their wanderings they came to Mount Hor beyond the mountains out of which the rose-red city of Petra was cut in later days, they found no wells of water.

Then the people again blamed Moses and Aaron for bringing them out of Egypt; and even they began to doubt Jahveh. But at last a Messenger came to them, saying:

'Strike the rock and water will come out. But because you have doubted Jahveh, neither of you shall enter the Promised Land.'

Sure enough, after the Israelites had rested and refreshed themselves at the miraculous spring of water, Aaron died upon Mount Hor, and his son Eleazar was made high priest in his place.

The mountain range of which Hor was the central peak was in the land of Edom, and its king would not let them pass through it. The Israelites were not strong enough to attack him, so Moses led them round the south of the range and up through the desert between the east side of Edom and the land of Uz.

On the way they fought with a Canaanite king called Arad and defeated him and destroyed his cities. And when the people complained again at the long, hard journey round the mountains to the head of the gulf where Aqaba now stands, fiery serpents were sent to bite them as a punishment.

So they passed to the north, conquering the Amorites on the way and destroying their cities. And they slew Og, the king of

For forty years the Israelites wandered through the wilderness

Bashan, the last of the giants, whose bedstead of iron was fifteen feet long and six wide, so huge was he.

When they came to Moab on the east side of the Jordan Balak, king of the Moabites, tried to stop them, sending his prophet Balaam to curse them. But the very ass on which Balaam rode turned round and warned its master in a human voice against standing against Jahveh's people. So Balak tried to win over the Israelites to become his subjects by sending Moabite girls to find husbands among them. But this brought a plague upon the Israelites, and they drove out the Moabite women after Phinehas the priest, the son of Eleazar, had killed one of them with the Israelite who had accepted her by thrusting a spear through them both.

Now, after forty years of wandering in the wilderness, the Israelites were on the very border of the Promised Land. But before they could enter it Jahveh sent his Messenger to Moses, saying:

'Go up into the mountains of Abarim at the foot of which the people of Israel are encamped, and look across the River Jordan to Jericho, the city of the Canaanites. Go to a high peak so that you can see all the plain of Jordan from the Dead Sea away to the north to the Sea of Galilee and across the river beyond Jericho to the high lands there, where Jerusalem, the holy city, shall be built. And when you have seen it, the Promised Land that shall belong to the Children of Israel, come down into the valley; for the day of your death has come and, like Aaron, you may not enter the Promised Land since even you have doubted the words and the might of Jahveh.'

Then Moses said: 'Since I may not lead my people into the land of Israel, let Jahveh choose a man to succeed me and proclaim his name to all the people so that they may follow him and obey his words, knowing that they come from Jahveh.'

And the Messenger answered: 'Take Joshua, the son of Nun, a man in whom the spirit of Jahveh shines brightly, and present him to the people. He shall take your place and lead them to victory in the Promised Land. And let him be anointed their ruler by Eleazar, the priest, who will stand to him as Aaron stood to you. Then hasten up to Nebo.'

So Moses led the Israelites down onto the plain of Moab, near the east bank of the River Jordan, and saw them safely encamped there. Then he gathered them together and told them the will of Jahveh, ending:

'When I am dead Joshua shall lead you across the Jordan into the land of Canaan. There you shall drive out all the inhabitants, or slaughter them if they resist. And you shall destroy temples and shrines and works of art, and take all the land for yourselves and colonize it and settle there. Be sure you drive out all the people whose home it is, for if you let any remain they will be like thorns in your sides, causing trouble when you have divided their land among yourselves.'

Then Moses went up to Nebo in the mountains of Moab and looked out over the Jordan valley from the Dead Sea to the Sea of Galilee, and over Jericho and the hills beyond where in days to come Jerusalem and Bethlehem were to be built, and right over the land even to the Great Sea beyond.

Then having seen all the Promised Land where the people of

Israel were to dwell so long as they were worthy of it, Moses died, being one hundred and twenty years old.

And the Israelites mourned for him for thirty days, and buried his body in a valley of the mountains of Moab. But no man knows to this day exactly where his grave is.

Book Four

THE PROMISED LAND

THE FALL OF JERICHO

When Moses was dead and buried, and the thirty days of mourning were over, Joshua made ready to lead the Israelites into the Promised Land of Canaan beyond the River Jordan.

But first of all he sent two men across as spies to get into the city of Jericho and discover all they could about its defences and see if there were any weak spots.

The two disguised themselves and crossed the river by night. In the morning they walked boldly through the fields for a few miles until they came to the high walls of Jericho which stood on a little hill near the western side of the long narrow plain that forms the Jordan valley.

They slipped quietly into the city and wandered about for some time, taking a room for the night in the house of a woman called Rahab.

However, the two strangers had been seen and suspected, and it was reported to the Governor of the city that spies, thought to be from Israel, had been followed and seen to go into a house built on the city wall which was a place of ill repute.

So the Governor sent soldiers to arrest them. But when they knocked on the door Rahab hid the two Israelites and said to the guard:

'Yes, there were two strangers who came to my house. I have no idea who or what they were, for in my business we ask no questions of our clients. As for where they are now, I only know that they left not long ago—as soon as it began to get dark. Probably you will catch them at the gate of the city if you hurry.'

Then the guard hastened out of Jericho and along the road to the ford over Jordan. But Rahab went up to where she had hidden the two Israelites under the piles of flax on the flat roof of the house, and said to them:

'The Governor's guards are looking for you. But I have sent them off to seek at the gate and down towards the river. I did not give you away to them, for I know that you of Israel are stronger than we of Jericho and will certainly conquer us. For we have heard what you did to the Amorites and their king, and to Og, the King of Bashan—and of the magic by which you passed dry-shod through the Red Sea but sent back the waters to drown Pharaoh and all his armies. So now, if I help you to escape out of Jericho, swear to me that when you conquer the city you will spare both me and all that is mine.'

Then they swore that she and all her house would be safe, and told her to hang a red cord out of her window when the attack came so that the Israelites would know which house to spare.

So she lowered a rope from her window, right down the outside of the wall of Jericho; and before they climbed down it she said:

'When you reach the foot of the wall, creep away in the darkness round to the west side and get away up into the mountains for a day or two until the Governor's men have given up looking for you. Then you may return under cover of darkness and cross the ford back to your own people.'

Then they made her swear not to breathe a word of their visit, and once again promised to spare her and her family if she proved true to them, and so made their escape.

When they returned to the Israelite camp several days later and told all their tale to Joshua he exclaimed:

'Truly Jahveh has delivered this people into our hands, for already they are all in mortal terror of us. Now we will set out over the Jordan and lay siege to Jericho.'

Next day the whole Israelite army moved down to the very edge of the Jordan, with all the rest of the people behind them, and encamped beside the stream a few miles from where it flowed into the Dead Sea.

Now the Jordan is not more than twenty yards wide, but deep and swift-flowing, and the Israelites wondered how they were to get across. But Jahveh had sent one of his Messengers to Joshua, who rose up before the people and said:

'Fast and pray today, for tomorrow Jahveh will work great wonders. When the morning comes form up in companies and follow the priests who carry the Ark of the Covenant, keeping a thousand yards behind it—and follow without fear wherever it goes.'

At dawn, accordingly, the Children of Israel formed up with all their goods and baggage animals and prepared to follow the priest as Joshua commanded. These were gathered in a compact body round those who carried the Ark—an oblong chest of acacia wood about four feet long by two wide and deep, carried on poles passed through rings at the four corners, and covered with the veil or curtain of badgers' skins and blue cloth which was set up as a tent to cover it when the Israelites were encamped.

As soon as the priests who carried the Ark, which contained the tablets and scrolls of the Law, came to the edge of the water, which was overflowing the banks on either side, it seemed to draw away from their feet. As they advanced the river ceased to flow from the north and banked up as the Red Sea had done. But the water on the side towards the south continued to flow into the Dead Sea until the whole bed of the river was exposed —a hard, dry hollow of sand and salt and clay, scattered with stones.

Across this the Israelites marched dryshod until all were over on the west bank. Then the water slid back into place and continued to flow on its way. But as they went one man from each of the twelve tribes by Joshua's order picked up from the river bed a stone as large as he could lift and carried it over with him. And when all were over and the people were encamped on the flat plain to the west of the river, Joshua caused the twelve stones to be set up as a memorial of the Jordan crossing to mark the place where the Israelites spent their first night in the Promised Land. And this site, between the Jordan and the city of Jericho, was called Gilgal.

When they heard of the crossing of Jordan by the Israelites, the Canaanites were afraid; and those who dwelt in the valley made haste to shut themselves up in the fortified city of Jericho and bar all the gates.

But the Israelites encamped at Gilgal and celebrated the Feast of the Passover while Joshua considered how to attack Jericho.

As he stood out on the plain between the camp and the city, wondering how to break into a place with such huge old walls, he saw a man with a drawn sword in his hand standing not far away towards Jericho.

'Who are you?' cried Joshua, drawing his own sword and advancing towards the stranger. 'Are you for us or one of our enemies?'

'I come as one of the captains of the Army of Jahveh,' answered the stranger, and Joshua realized suddenly that it was a Messenger from heaven, and fell on his face before him and did him reverence, saying: 'I am no better than a servant: tell me the commands of Jahveh.'

And the Messenger of Jahveh said: 'First take off your shoes, for the place where you stand is holy.'

Joshua did so, and the Messenger said: 'Now listen how

THE FALL OF JERICHO

Jahveh will give Jericho into your hands.' And he went on with his message, and then vanished as suddenly as he had come.

Then Joshua hastened back to the Israelite camp and issued his commands. And next morning the armed men set out for Jericho and all the people behind them, and in their midst the priests carrying the Ark of the Covenant, and in front of it seven more priests carrying trumpets made of rams' horns.

As they marched round the city of Jericho the priests blew their trumpets. But Joshua said to the people: 'Do not shout, nor make any noise with your voices, nor speak a single word until the appointed day when I shall bid you shout—and then you shall let them have it for all you are worth.'

So the silent army marched round the city before and behind the group of priests who blew their trumpets, and returned to their camp without making any attempt to attack.

Each day for six days they made their strange progress round Jericho, until the Canaanites inside felt as if some terrible spell was being woven about them.

Early on the morning of the seventh day Joshua gathered the people again and said:

'This day you shall march seven times round the city in silence. But on the seventh round when I give the word, all shout, and let the priests blow their trumpets, until the Canaanites are deafened with the din. And Jahveh will deliver Jericho into your hands. Rush in and slay all the inhabitants, except the woman Rahab and her family, and destroy the city, and all things in it save only the silver and gold and brass and iron. Bring these into the treasury to be dedicated to Jahveh. But take nothing else. For the city is accursed, and a curse will fall on anyone who takes so much as a single garment from Jericho, or anything for himself.'

So the Israelites marched seven times round the city; and on the seventh round when they came to the oldest and highest portion of the wall Joshua bade them halt. Then he gave the signal: the priests blew their trumpets with all the power of their lungs, and the soldiers and people shouted with a great shrill cry.

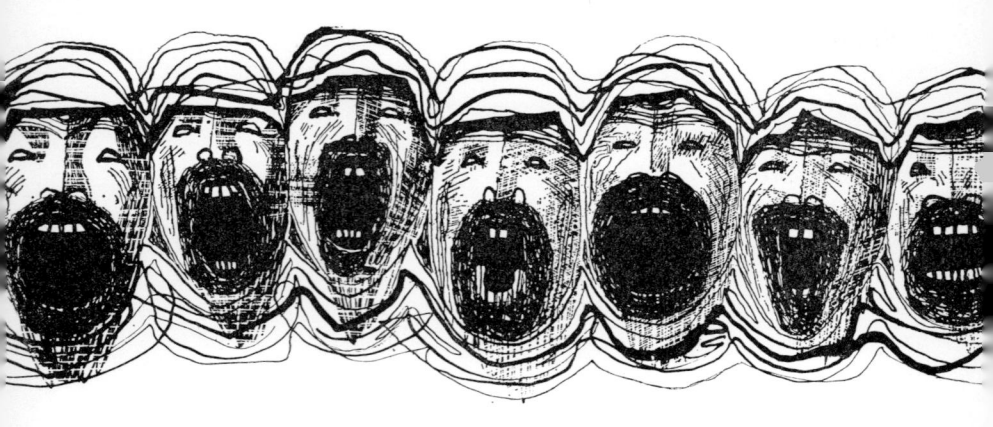

They shouted with a great shrill cry

And at the deafening sound a great section of the wall was shivered from top to bottom, split away from the rest and came crashing down.

'Now!' cried Joshua. 'In and slay, and spare not!'

Then the army of the Israelites rushed in through the gap in the wall and slew the terrified Canaanites, men, women and children, sparing none. And they killed all the cattle and sheep and asses, and destroyed everything in the city except the gold and silver and iron and brass which they handed over to the priests.

But they saved Rahab, with her father and mother and brothers, and all their possessions, and set them free outside the camp of Israel.

Then they burned the city to the ground and destroyed the remaining walls, and left it a heap of ruins over which Joshua pronounced a curse on any who should try to rebuild it.

Flushed with victory, Joshua sent forward an army of about three thousand men to take the city of Ai up in the hills twelve miles to the north-west: for his spies had told him that it had no great walls like those at Jericho, and was poorly defended.

'Go up to Ai,' commanded Joshua, 'and sack the city, and bring back all the inhabitants as slaves.'

THE FALL OF JERICHO

But the Canaanites were ready for the invaders. They attacked them so fiercely that a number of the Israelites were killed, and the rest they chased all the way back to Jericho.

Then the people of Israel were seized with panic, and Joshua tore his clothes and rolled on the ground, crying aloud to Jahveh:

'Why have you brought the people all this way to be destroyed by the Canaanites? We would have been quite happy on the other side of Jordan which we had taken from the Moabites. But now the rest of the Canaanites will hear about our defeat, and surround us and kill us all!'

This, however, was not Jahveh's will, and his word came to Joshua: 'This defeat has befallen Israel because my commands have been disobeyed. One of you has taken some of the spoils of Jericho for himself, when I commanded that all save the priests' treasures were to be destroyed. Therefore this curse has fallen upon you and cannot be lifted until you find the sinner and destroy with fire him, his family, all his possessions—and the accursed spoils of Jericho.'

As soon as this was implanted in Joshua's mind he called together all the people of Israel and caused them to pass in front of him tribe by tribe. And he was moved to choose the tribe of Judah; and from the tribe of Judah the family of the Zarhites; and from the family of the Zarhites the old man Zabdi was taken. Then all Zabdi's descendants were examined one by one, and his grandson Achan was revealed as the sinner.

Then Joshua said to him gently: 'My son, praise Jahveh, and make your confession to him. And tell me what you have done: do not hide it from me.'

'I have sinned indeed,' answered Achan sadly, 'for when I saw among the spoils of Jericho a beautiful Babylonian garment, and two hundred shekels of silver and a wedge of gold weighing two shekels, I longed for these so much that I took them and hid them under the floor of my tent.'

At once Joshua sent messengers to Achan's tent who dug into the ground in the middle of it and found the garment and eight pounds weight of silver and the two of gold. They brought these to Joshua and laid them before him.

Then Joshua and all the people took Achan and the silver and the garment and the wedge of gold, and brought them to a nearby valley. They brought also Achan's sons and his daughters, his oxen and his asses, his sheep and his tent.

Then Joshua cried: 'You, Achan, have brought all this trouble on us by disobeying Jahveh's commands which I proclaimed to you all before the fall of Jericho. It is only right that you should be troubled today.'

And thereupon, at Joshua's orders, the Israelites stoned Achan and his sons and daughters, and afterwards burned them to ashes, together with all his possessions, including the contraband from Jericho. Then they heaped up a great pile of rocks over the ashes, and named the place Achor, the Valley of Trouble.

Then Joshua sent thirty thousand men by night to hide in a narrow valley just behind the city of Ai. And he led the rest of the Israelites against the main gates of the city, having instructed both bodies very carefully what to do.

When morning dawned the King of Ai saw the Israelite army in front of his city. Remembering how easily he had defeated the first invaders, he led out all his forces to attack them, knowing nothing of the thirty thousand men lying in ambush behind him.

Almost at once the Israelites cried out as if in terror and turned to flee. And the Canaanites of Ai, thinking they had defeated them again, began to chase them through the mountains and the wilderness towards the Jordan valley.

When they were far enough away Joshua sprang upon a rock visible from behind Ai and waved his spear so that the sunlight flashed on its blade. At once the Israelites hiding in the valley saw the signal and poured into undefended Ai from behind.

They took the city without any difficulty and set it on fire. Then they rushed out after the Canaanite army, and Joshua turned to give battle from his side.

When they saw the smoke rising from their city, the Canaanites turned back in panic. But before they could escape the two armies of Israelites had surrounded them; and they showed no mercy but slew them all to the last man, save only for the King of Ai who was brought as a prisoner to Joshua.

Then by Joshua's command the Israelites slaughtered all the other inhabitants of Ai until not one remained. But they took all the spoil from the city, with all the flocks and herds, and divided it among themselves.

As for the King of Ai, Joshua caused him to be hanged on a tree. And that night he had his body cut down and flung on the ground in the gateway of the city, and a mound of stones piled over it in memory of the Israelites' triumph.

'THE SWORD OF THE LORD AND OF GIDEON'

AFTER Jericho and Ai had fallen the Israelites began to settle on the west side of the River Jordan. But the country was by no means conquered, and it took another twenty-five years before Jerusalem was taken and the people were able to settle down and live in peace.

Joshua died soon after the taking of Jerusalem, and for nearly a hundred years after his death there were no major wars, though the Israelites continued to drive out the inhabitants of Canaan and colonize the land themselves—the country which they now began to call the land of Israel.

But peace and prosperity, and the feeling of power, had its usual bad effect on the Israelites. In spite of all that Jahveh had done for them, and of the high destiny promised to their nation if only they would worship one God, the Israelites began to break the first and second commandments given to Moses.

They worshipped Baal and Ashtoreth, the gods of the Canaanites, and made images of them and practised the various heathen rites necessary to their services.

In anger Jahveh sent his Messenger to warn the Israelites of punishment to come if they did not mend their ways and remember the Covenant of Moses. But only a few of the leaders took the warning to heart. These leaders elected rulers or judges to judge the people of Israel and try to keep them to the paths of righteousness.

But they did not succeed. Therefore Jahveh allowed the Israelites to be ruled by various alien kings for short periods; and each time the people repented, and were allowed to throw off the foreign yoke. But each time they were free they fell again into temptation, and offered human sacrifice to Baal or Moloch, and danced naked in the groves with the priestesses of Astarte and Ashtoreth.

Then Jabin, King of the Canaanites, set himself up to rule Israel, and the people were afraid to rebel, for he had a great army and nine hundred iron chariots. For twenty years he ruled as a dictator in Israel until Jahveh took pity on the sufferings of the people and accepted their repentance.

Then he sent his Messenger to Deborah the prophetess, and she spoke the words of Jahveh to a certain captain of the Israelites called Barak, saying:

'Take ten thousand warriors of Israel and lead them secretly to Mount Tabor. And I will persuade Sisera, Jabin's general, to lead his army to the River Kishon, with all his chariots. There you may ambush them and rush down upon them from above, and slay them all.'

'If you will come with us, then I will lead the army,' said Barak. 'But if you will not come I do not stir a step.'

'Indeed, I will come, if you do not have faith in my words alone,' answered Deborah. 'But then the supreme honour of the victory will not be yours, for Sisera shall fall by the hands of a woman.'

So Deborah the prophetess went with Barak and his army to Mount Tabor to the north of Palestine near the Sea of Galilee. But she sent Heber the Kenite to Sisera to deceive him; for Heber was Sisera's trusted friend, but was in fact a secret agent of the Israelites.

'Barak plans war against you,' Heber told Sisera. 'He has led a small force in the direction of Mount Tabor. But I can show you how to set an ambush into which he and all his men cannot help falling—and, as they are few and you are many, you may slaughter them all.'

So Sisera gathered together his men and chariots and marched to the River Kishon where there was a ford near the slopes of Mount Tabor.

Meanwhile Barak and his army were in hiding above the ford. And Deborah said: 'This is the moment of which I prophesied: Jahveh has delivered the Canaanites into your hand. Rise up and smite them!'

So Barak charged suddenly down the mountainside with his ten thousand men and took the Canaanites by surprise and conquered and slew and scattered them, seizing all their iron chariots.

Sisera, however, escaped from the battle on foot and fled for refuge to the tent of Heber the Kenite, his friend. Heber was not there, but his wife Jael came out to welcome Sisera, crying:

'Come in quickly, my lord—come into my tent and do not be afraid. I will hide you and none of your enemies will suspect that you are here.'

So Sisera turned thankfully into Jael's tent and lay down on the floor hidden under a blanket.

Presently he begged for a drink, and she gave him milk, and covered him up once more. Then Israelites began to pass through the camp, and Sisera whispered:

'Stand in the door of the tent, and when anyone asks if there is anybody in the tent, say that your husband is away and no one else is here.'

So Jael stood in the doorway and kept passers-by from coming in until Sisera, feeling safe from discovery, and being very tired after the battle and his flight, fell asleep.

As soon as she heard him snoring, Jael took a sharp tent peg like a great nail and a hammer and went softly up to him. Sisera did not stir, and so with a few swift blows of the hammer she drove the tent peg through his head and nailed him to the ground with it.

Presently Barak reached Heber's camp in pursuit of Sisera, and Jael came out of the tent to meet him.

'Come in here,' she said. 'Come and let me show you the man you are looking for.'

Then Barak came into the tent, and there lay Sisera dead with the tent peg driven through his head.

After this Barak and Deborah sang a great song of triumph to the glory of Jahveh and in praise of Israel. The people rejoiced in

There lay Sisera dead with the tent peg driven through his head

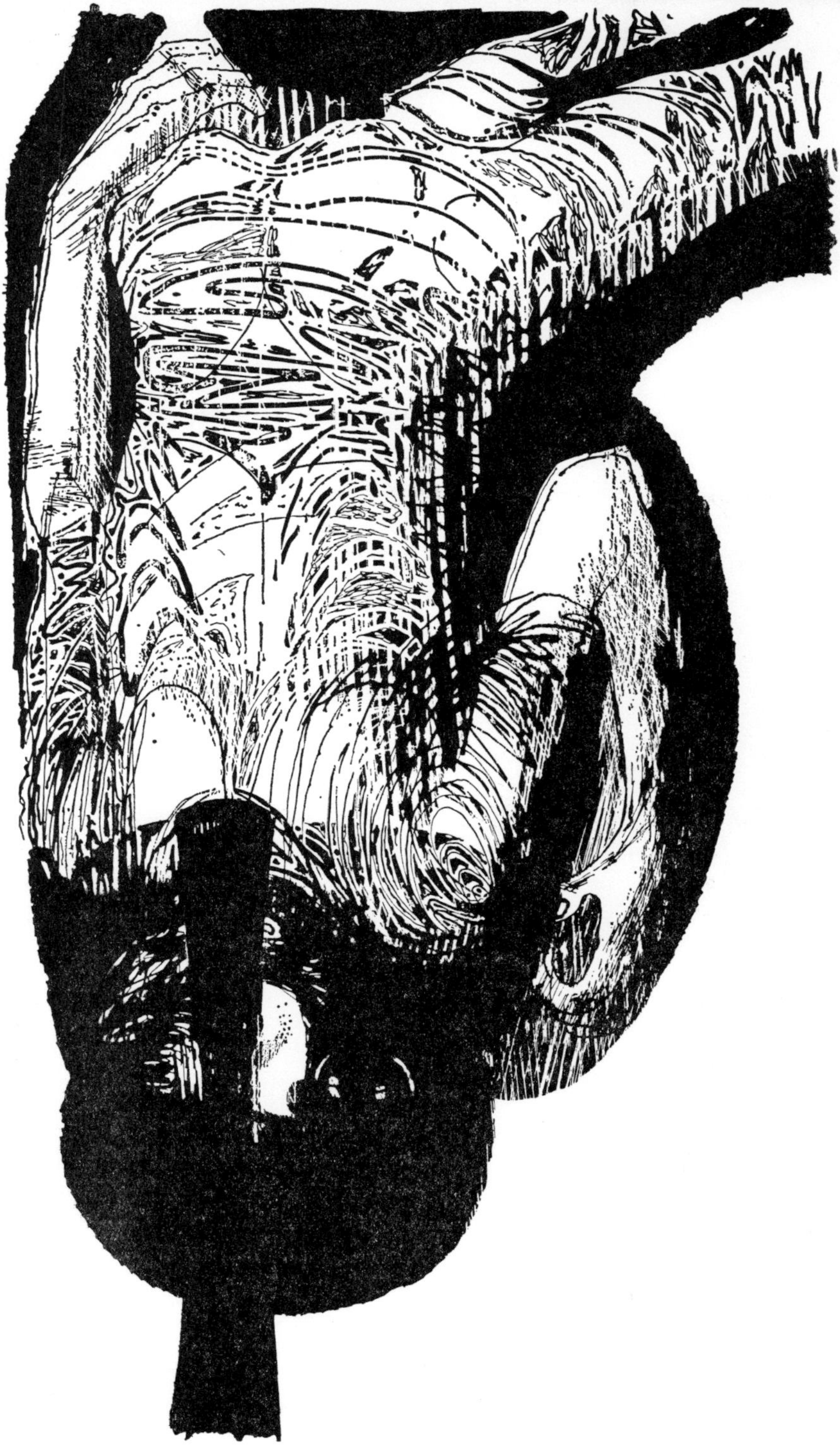

the victory and gave thanks to Jahveh for a little while; but they soon lapsed back into the easy worship of the gods of their Canaanite wives, and celebrated the rites of Baal and Ashtoreth once more.

Then came the Midianites, and overran Israel, and destroyed the harvest and many of the flocks and herds. And those of the Israelites whose lands were overrun fled to the caves in the mountains above the Dead Sea and hid there as if they had been wolves or foxes.

But Jahveh sent his Messenger to a place called Ophrah some twenty-five miles to the north of Jerusalem and of the Dead Sea. And this angel sat himself down under an oak tree near where a certain Israelite warrior called Gideon, the son of Joash, was threshing his corn behind a winepress to hide it from the Midianites.

'Jahveh shows favour towards you, Gideon, mighty man of valour,' said the Messenger.

'O my lord,' answered Gideon, 'if Jahveh is with any of us, why have all these troubles befallen his people? And where are all the wonders of which our fathers have told us of how Jahveh saved our people from Pharaoh and brought them out of the land of Egypt and guarded them for forty years in the wilderness, until they reached the Promised Land? Surely he has forgotten us and given us over as slaves to the Midianites!'

'Go strongly forward and save these your people from the Midianites,' said the Messenger, 'for Jahveh has sent you.'

'How can I save Israel?' asked Gideon. 'My family is poor, and I am the least important member of it.'

'Jahveh will indeed be with you and help you,' the Messenger assured him. But Gideon still doubted, and said to the angel:

'If I have indeed found favour in Jahveh's sight, so that he has chosen me to lead Israel against the Midianites, I beg you to show me a sign that you indeed come from him.'

'Fetch out your usual sacrifice to Jahveh and lay it on this rock here,' commanded the Messenger.

Gideon made haste into his dwelling and prepared a kid and unleavened cakes made of flour. He brought out the kid and cakes and laid them on the flat rock.

Then the Messenger touched the flesh and the cakes with the end of the staff which he carried in his hand, and at once fire rose up out of the rock and burned the kid and the cakes to ashes. And in the same flash of fire and smoke the Messenger vanished.

Gideon realized that he had indeed received a true message from Jahveh, and as soon as he had built an altar in his honour, he set out to do the various things the Messenger had commanded him.

That very night he and ten faithful followers destroyed the altar of Baal and cut down the grove round about it, and sacrificed a bullock to Jahveh.

In the morning the men of Ophrah and the district round about came in a great fear and fury to Joash, saying: 'Bring out your son so that we may kill him as a punishment for destroying the altar of Baal and cutting down the sacred grove of our god.'

But Joash said to the Israelites of Ophrah: 'Would you kill one of our own people on account of Baal? If Baal is a true god let him prove it by blasting my son with the fire of his anger.'

This seemed fair to the Israelites, and they called upon Baal to blast Gideon. But as Baal did nothing about it, they realized how foolish they had been, and made no further attempt to punish Gideon.

But Gideon, hearing that the Midianites had persuaded the Amalekites to help them and were preparing to overrun and enslave all Israel, went about the land blowing a trumpet to gather the men of war together in defence of their liberty.

Many gathered together; but when he learned how strong and vast were the hosts of the Midianites and Amalekites, Gideon was afraid, and he cried to Jahveh, saying:

'If you will indeed save Israel by my hand, give me another proof! I will put this fleece from a lamb on the ground tonight: if the earth is dry all round it and the fleece is wet tomorrow, I will take that as a sign.'

Next morning the earth was dry and hard: not a drop of dew had fallen during the night. But when Gideon picked up the fleece, he wrung a bowlful of dew out of it. He was afraid still, however, and called to Jahveh once more:

'If indeed this is a true sign, give me one more—and do not be angry at my caution. Tomorrow let the earth be wet but the fleece dry!'

When Gideon came out next morning the grass was drenched with dew. But there was not one scrap of moisture in the fleece which lay in the wettest place: it was as dry as if it had hung by the fire all night.

Then Gideon doubted no more. He set up his standard beside the Well of Harod, and the Israelites gathered about him to the number of thirty-two thousand, all armed and ready to attack the Midianites and their allies who were encamped below them in the valley of Moreh.

But the message came to Gideon that Jahveh would show his power by scattering the Midianites at the hands of a far smaller army. So Gideon proclaimed to the Israelites: 'Anyone who is afraid, or fears lest we should be defeated, let him go away from Mount Gilead.' And over two-thirds of the Israelites departed in a hurry, leaving only ten thousand men.

Once again, however, the message of Jahveh came to Gideon: 'Your army is still too big. Bring them to the water to drink, and take careful note of how they do so. Those who cup the water in their hands and lap set on one side; and those who bend their faces right down into the water to suck it up set on the other side. Those who lap shall go with you and conquer the Midianites; but those who bend down and set their lips to the water you shall send home.'

Of the ten thousand only three hundred men cupped their hands and lapped the water out of them—and with these alone Gideon set out to conquer the Midianites.

They camped on the slope of Mount Gilead, above but out of sight of the Midianites in the valley. And as soon as it was dark Gideon and his squire Phurah stole down to spy on the enemy.

Soon they found the Midianites camped along the valley—and their numbers were as countless as the hosts of locusts Moses had summoned to destroy the crops of the Egyptians, and their camels seemed as many as the sands on the seashore.

By and by Gideon and Phurah overheard two men sitting beside a camp-fire. One of them had just woken up, and he said to his companion:

'I have had such a strange dream. It seemed as if a large loaf of barley bread came tumbling down into our army; and it came into a tent and struck it, and at once the whole tent collapsed in ruins.'

'It seems to me', said the other Midianite, shivering, 'that the barley cake must mean the sword of Gideon the son of Joash, and as if Jahveh had delivered Midian and all the host into his hand.'

When Gideon heard this he took it as a sign from Jahveh, and hastened back rejoicing to the Israelite camp where he roused the three hundred men, saying:

'The time has come to attack—for Jahveh has delivered the Midianites into our hands.'

When they were armed he divided them into three companies of a hundred men each, telling each man to take in his hands a trumpet, an empty pitcher and a flaming torch, and to hide the flaming torch in the pitcher.

'Watch and listen to me,' he cautioned them, 'and do exactly as I do. When I blow my own trumpet, you blow yours and shout loudly: "The sword of the Lord and of Gideon." '

So they stole down the hill silently in the darkness until they came to the camp of the Midianites at about the time of the middle watch, when the sentries were just being changed.

Then, following Gideon's example, the three hundred Israelites blew their trumpets and broke the pitchers and charged, waving the torches and shouting: 'The sword of the Lord and of Gideon!'

Now Gideon had manœuvred them into position all round the camp: and at the sudden blast of trumpets and flashing of torches all round them, the Midianites thought that they were surrounded by a gigantic host—and panicked.

They flung down their arms and fled in every direction, while the ruthless Israelites slaughtered them on all sides, slaying thousands until only a remnant was able to escape, leaving all their possessions behind.

The Israelites captured the two princes of the Midianites and hacked them to pieces without mercy, and brought their heads to Gideon. And he led his three hundred, weary but triumphant, across the Jordan, and subdued all the land with great slaughter.

Then for forty years Israel was at peace. The people wished to make Gideon their king, but he said:

'I will not rule over you: Jahveh alone is your ruler, and he has given you this victory. But if you would reward me for leading you in this campaign, let each man give me the gold earrings which he has taken from the Midianites whom he has slain.'

So the Israelites spread a robe on the ground and flung the golden earrings on to it willingly; and Gideon became a rich man, for the weight of the gold that became his was more than seventy pounds.

With this wealth Gideon was able to have many wives; and when he died at a ripe old age he was the father of seventy sons.

SAMSON AND THE PHILISTINES

So LONG as Gideon lived the Israelites did not stray far from the worship of God. But after his death they began to turn once more to the easy and self-indulgent religion of Baal and Ashtoreth. Consequently Jahveh sent the Ammonites against them, and for many years they led an uneasy existence with an enemy constantly penetrating deep into their lands with commandos and guerrilla bands striving to free Canaan from its Israelite invaders.

At last they found a man called Jephthah to be their general, mighty of valour and a great warrior. For a long time he had dwelt alone on the edge of the desert of Tob to the north-east of the lands which the Israelites had occupied; for his mother was a wicked and immoral woman, and his half-brothers had driven him out of his home.

But in their despair at the inroads which the Ammonites were making the elders of Gilead went to find Jephthah and begged him to gather an army and lead it against the enemy.

'Did not you and my brothers hate and despise me because of my mother's way of life?' asked Jephthah bitterly, when the embassy found him. 'Did not you hate me so much that you drove me out of my home to live here in the wilderness? Do you not come to ask my help now only because you are in trouble and think that I can help you?'

'We must admit that all you say is true,' answered the elders. 'But the need of Israel is desperate, and we believe that you alone can help us. Therefore we have come to ask you to be our leader.'

'If you bring me home to fight against the Ammonites, and by

Jahveh's will I manage to conquer them, will you still have me as your leader?' asked Jephthah.

'We swear before Jahveh and on behalf of all the Israelites of Gilead that you shall indeed rule over us for the rest of your life, if you defeat the Ammonites,' said the elders. 'May Jahveh be witness to our words and slay us all if we break them.'

So Jephthah returned to Gilead and gathered together the hosts of Israel. First of all he sent ambassadors to the King of the Ammonites asking him why he made war on Israel and suggesting that he withdrew his troops and made peace. But when the king replied that there could be no peace until Israel gave up all the lands they had taken from the Ammonites and their allies, Jephthah marched at once from Gilead to Mizpah to do battle with him.

Before he set out, however, Jephthah made a solemn vow before all the people, saying:

'I swear in the sight of Jahveh and of you all that if Jahveh gives me the victory over the Ammonites I will sacrifice to him as a burnt offering whatsoever thing comes out of my door first to meet me when I return after the battle.'

Then Jephthah set out with his army; and he met the Ammonites and defeated them and destroyed twenty of their cities, together with their vineyards, and slaughtered so many thousands of them that the survivors were glad to make peace with Israel at any price and became their subjects.

Jephthah marched back to Mizpah in triumph when the war was over and came to his house. As he reached it his daughter came dancing out to meet him. Now she was his only child, for he had no other son or daughter, and he loved her above all things on earth.

When he saw her Jephthah remembered his oath. Then he wept and tore his clothes, and cried:

'Alas, alas, my daughter, you have brought me to uttermost woe and misery. I have made a vow to Jahveh and I cannot go back on my word, for if Jahveh did not slay me the people would.'

His daughter came dancing out to meet him

'Father, if you have made a vow to Jahveh which concerns me', said his daughter, 'I beg you to keep it. For Jahveh has taken vengeance on the Ammonites at your hand, and I am a small sacrifice for such a victory.'

Even when he told her what he had vowed Jephthah's daughter said only: 'Give me two months to mourn up on the mountains with the other maidens of Israel, and then I will go willingly to my death.'

So Jephthah's daughter spent two months with the maidens of

Israel, mourning upon the mountains that her life was unfulfilled since she was to die unmarried.

Then she returned to Mizpah, and Jephthah kept his vow, sacrificing her to Jahveh and burning her body to ashes upon the altar.

But in memory of Jephthah's daughter the maidens of Israel mourned for ever after for four days in each year upon the mountains of Gilead.

As for Jephthah, he continued the war against the enemies of Israel and was everywhere triumphant. He seemed so invincible that one group of invaders pretended to be Israelites so as to avoid falling victim to his wrath. However, he ordered all the inhabitants of their district to cross the Jordan at a particular ford, and to give the password which was 'Shibboleth'. The true Israelites could pronounce this properly, but the pretended ones could not get their tongues round it—and Jephthah caused anyone who could not say 'Shibboleth' to be executed immediately. Forty-two thousand were identified and slain in this way.

Jephthah ruled Israel for only six years and then died.

There was peace in Israel for some years, until they fell once again into the sin of idolatry, worshipping Baal and Ashtoreth once more. And this time the enemies sent to punish them were the Philistines—the strongest and most powerful of the peoples who dwelt in Palestine, and at one time the rulers of the whole country —which was indeed named after them, for Palestine is the English form of the name for the place where the Philistines lived.

But even as he was always ready to punish the Israelites when they failed in their great destiny as the Chosen People, so Jahveh had ever a deliverer waiting to save them when they were ready to continue once more towards the high purpose for which they were protected so specially.

Even before Jephthah had been summoned to overthrow the Ammonites there dwelt in the village of Zorah, a dozen miles to the west of Jerusalem, an Israelite of the tribe of Dan whose name was Manoah.

He and his wife had no children. But one day a Messenger from Jahveh appeared, suddenly before her and said:

'Wife of Manoah, you are childless. But you shall bear a son to be the deliverer of Israel from the Philistines. He shall be dedicated to the service of Jahveh from the day of his birth to the day of his death, and in token of this he must never cut his hair.'

When the Messenger had gone Manoah's wife ran to her husband and told him what had happened. 'It was a holy man,' she said, 'but his face shone as if he had been one of Jahveh's angels.'

Then Manoah prayed to Jahveh, saying: 'Send your Messenger —if a Messenger from heaven it was indeed—to me also, that we may surely know whether my wife has been deceived or has indeed been told of things to come.'

And Jahveh sent his Messenger again when Manoah and his wife were in the fields next day, and Manoah's wife exclaimed:

'This is the same holy man who met me yesterday and told me that I should bear a son.'

'Are you indeed the man who spoke with my wife yesterday?' asked Manoah.

'I am he,' answered the Messenger, 'and I am come to tell you all that you must do. From this day your wife must drink no wine nor other strong drink, nor eat unclean food. And when your son is born he too must do likewise; for he must be a Nazarite—a man dedicated to Jahveh—all his life, never cutting his hair nor drinking wine nor spirits, nor eating unconsecrated flesh.'

'All this we will do,' said Manoah, 'but now come to my tent, I beg you, and eat of my bread.'

'That I may not do,' answered the Messenger, 'but I will stand beside you while you sacrifice a kid to Jahveh.'

So Manoah killed a young goat, built an altar, made a fire upon it and set the flesh of the kid in the midst of the flames. The Messenger raised his arms and the flames shot suddenly up into the sky so that sacrifice and sacrificial fire were consumed to ashes in a moment. And the Messenger went up to heaven with the flame, so that Manoah and his wife knew that he was indeed an angel sent to them by Jahveh. And they fell upon their faces and worshipped.

In due time Manoah's wife bore a son who was named Samson. And the child grew into a boy and into a young man—the strongest and the handsomest man that had been seen in Israel.

Being young and lusty, Samson went one day across the valley to Timnath where dwelt a group of Philistines. And he saw a pretty Philistine girl and immediately fell in love with her.

Returning home, he said to his father: 'I have seen a woman, a Philistine, in Timnath, whom I desire. Therefore I would like you to get her for me to be my wife.'

'Can you not find a woman among the people of Israel to be your wife?' said Manoah. 'Surely you do not mean to marry one of our enemies, a worshipper of the false god Dagon?'

But Samson insisted. So Manoah and his wife set off for Timnath to see if they could buy the young woman from her parents to be Samson's wife.

Presently Samson set out to follow them, and when he came to the outlying vineyards of Timnath he met a young lion who began to roar savagely at him.

Samson was not in the least afraid. But when the lion sprang at him he seized it in his bare hands and tore it in half as if it had been a kid. Then he flung the lion's body to the ground and went on into Timnath as if nothing had happened—and indeed he did not think it worth mentioning to anyone.

Samson liked the Philistine girl even more after his visit to Timnath, and his parents came to an arrangement with hers over bride price.

As he walked back to Mizpah by himself Samson passed the remains of the lion which he had killed and noticed to his surprise that a swarm of bees had made their nest in it. The honeycomb was dripping with honey, so he broke off a piece of it and went on his way munching happily, and gave what was left to his parents—though he did not tell them about the queer place in which he had found it.

All was now arranged for the wedding, and they set out again for Timnath with such things as were needed for the marriage feast.

Manoah was still grumbling about the high bride price, however, and at the feast Samson said suddenly to the thirty young men whom the Philistines had invited according to custom:

'I will ask you a riddle, and if you can solve it within seven days I will give to each of you a new tunic and a new cloak. But if you cannot solve it in that time each of you must give the same forfeit to me.'

'Agreed!' they cried. 'Ask us the riddle and we'll solve it!'

'Here it is!' cried Samson. ' "Out of the eater came forth meat, and out of the strong came forth sweetness." '

Not one of them could think of the answer; and during the next three days not one of them was able to do so.

Then they went privately to Samson's wife and said: 'Persuade your husband to tell you the answer to the riddle, and then tell it to us. Otherwise we will come and burn you and your father's house with fire—for you invited us to the wedding only so that you might rob us!'

So Samson's wife went to him in tears, sobbing: 'You do not really love me! You have asked my people a riddle, and you keep the answer even from me!'

'I have not told it to anyone, not even my father and mother,' said Samson, 'and I do not mean to tell it even to you.'

But she wept and cajoled and made his life a misery for the remaining days and nights of the feast, until at last he told her the answer—which she at once passed on to the thirty Philistine youths.

Therefore before the sun went down on the seventh day they were able to come to Samson and say:

'What is sweeter than honey? And what is stronger than a lion?'

Samson realized at once how they had discovered the answer,

and in a tremendous rage he seized his weapons and set off for Ashkelon, a stronghold of the Philistines, fifteen or more miles away. There he slew thirty men and took their tunics and cloaks, which he carried back to Timnath and gave to the young men who had solved his riddle by threatening his wife.

Then, still in a great rage, he returned home to Mizpah, leaving his wife behind with her father—who promptly gave her to Samson's companion, who had acted as best man at the wedding.

Not long after this, at the time when the wheat harvest was ripening, Samson's anger had cooled down and he set out for Timnath to visit his wife.

When he reached the house, however, her father met him at the door, saying:

'You cannot go into her room, for she is there with her husband. Thinking that you hated her, I married her off at once to your companion. But there is no need to be angry or disappointed: her younger sister is more beautiful than she is, and you may have her instead.'

'I shall be revenged on you and all the Philistines!' shouted Samson. 'And now I have a good excuse for whatever I do to them!'

So saying, he stormed back towards Mizpah, planning revenge. This he achieved by catching three hundred foxes, tying them together in couples by the tails and hanging a burning brand to each pair of brushes. Then he let the foxes loose in the cornfields of the Philistines, and the maddened creatures ran hither and thither through the standing corn and among the shocks of wheat which had already been cut and tied into sheaves and stooked. Wherever they went they set the corn on fire, and most of the harvest for miles round was destroyed.

Then the Philistines asked who had done this terrible damage; and when they found that it was Samson, the son-in-law of the Timnite, because he had taken his wife and given her to another man, they surrounded the house and burned both Samson's wife and her father to ashes.

But Samson rushed upon them, crying: 'For what you have done I will be revenged upon you, and after that let there be peace between us.'

And he smote them hip and thigh, slaying a huge number. Then he retired to the Mount of Etam and dwelt in a cave at the top of it from which he could see in every direction, to guard against surprise.

The Philistines felt that they could not compete with Samson. But they tried a surer way. They gathered an army and overran all those parts of Israel round Etam and Mizpah where the tribe of Judah had settled. And the Israelites of Judah said:

'Why have you come against us in arms? We have done you no harm, and were living peacefully under your rule.'

They answered: 'We have come to demand that Samson be given up to us bound hand and foot so that we may punish him for all the evil he has done us. Give him to us, or else we will punish all of you as well.'

Then the men of Judah sent an army of three thousand men to surround the top of Etam and seize Samson; and they said to him:

'Surely you realize that the Philistines are our masters and rule over us? Why have you behaved like this? You must realize how grievously we are likely to suffer for what you have done.'

'I only took just vengeance on them for what they had done to me,' answered Samson.

'Nevertheless we must bind you and give you up to the Philistines,' they said.

'You are welcome to do so', answered Samson, 'if you will first swear to do me no other harm yourselves, but simply to bind me and hand me over.'

'Agreed,' they answered. 'We swear not to kill you nor harm you in any way, but simply to tie you up and give you to the Philistines.'

So they bound Samson with two new ropes and brought him down from Etam and handed him over to the Philistines.

As soon as they had taken him away from the men of Judah, they gathered round him to put him to a cruel death. But the strength of Jahveh came upon him and the ropes which bound his arms seemed no stronger than flax that has been burnt with fire.

With one heave of his mighty shoulders Samson burst all the bonds that held him. Then, looking about for a weapon, he found the jawbone of an ass that had but lately died. This he snatched up and set upon the Philistines so fiercely that he slew a thousand of them with it before the rest were able to turn and fly.

Then he flung away the jawbone and returned to his own people who made much of him, now that he had routed the Philistines. And Samson became the ruler of Israel for the next twenty years, the Philistines being so frightened of him that they dared not do anything against him or the Israelites, or try to enforce their sway over them.

Once they thought they had caught him, when Samson wandered into their city of Gaza near the sea coast and to visit there a woman whom he loved. When they discovered he was in the city the Philistines shut all the gates and placed guards at each of them with instructions to cut him down in the morning when he tried to get out.

But Samson rose at midnight, came down to the nearest gate and, finding it barred, charged through it taking both halves of the gate, with the posts and all, on his shoulders and far away into the darkness to dump them on a nearby hill top before returning home.

In the end, however, he fell violently in love with a very beautiful Philistine woman called Delilah who lived in the valley of Sorek between Mizpah and Gaza.

The lords of the Philistines were delighted when they heard of this, and they said to Delilah:

'Make Samson infatuated with you, and then tease him and cajole him and plague him into telling you where his great strength lies and how we may overcome him. And if you betray him into our power we will each one of us give you eleven hundred pieces of silver.'

So Delilah married Samson, and made him very happy except

that she was for ever trying to persuade him to tell her the secret of his amazing strength and how he could be overcome.

At last, in a moment of pique, he exclaimed: 'All right, I'll tell you. I would be powerless if I were bound with seven new, wet cords that had never been dried or used before. If I were tied up with them I would be no stronger than any other man.'

Next day she told the lords of the Philistines, and they brought her the seven new cords.

And that night, when she had lulled him to sleep, Delilah bound Samson with the cords. Then she cried out:

'Samson! Samson! The Philistines are upon you!'

With a start Samson woke and leapt to his feet, breaking the seven cords as if they had been no more than cotton.

Then Delilah wept and refused to be comforted, sobbing: 'You don't love me at all! You mock me and tell me lies! If you love me tell me where your strength lies and how you could be bound with bonds that you could not break.'

'You mistook what I told you,' said Samson at last. 'I said new ropes, not mere cords. Now stop crying and come back to bed.'

The following night Delilah bound her husband with seven strong ropes that had never before been used. Then once more she woke him by crying:

'Samson! Samson! The Philistines are upon you!'

Up he leapt as before, the ropes breaking beneath his giant muscles, as if they had been no more than flax—and Delilah again had recourse to tears and reproaches, sobbing:

'Now I know how true your love is! As true as these lies you have been telling me.' And she went on until Samson exclaimed:

'All right. I'll tell you my secret. Weave the seven locks of my hair into a web on a weaver's beam and I will become as weak as any ordinary man.'

That night Delilah made sure that Samson was deeply asleep, and then she wove his hair into a web and cried:

'Samson! Samson! The Philistines are upon you!'

Up he sprang and tore out of the room with the web and the

beam and the loom itself swinging behind him on his long hair as if he did not notice them.

Day and night after this Delilah coaxed and wheedled Samson, saying again and again that he could not love her if he did not trust her. And she worked him up into such a state of weariness and frustration that at last he said:

'Well, since you say that you love me so much, and for the sake of a little peace—for you are worrying me to death—I will tell you the truth. I have been a Nazarite, vowed to Jahveh, since my birth, and neither razor nor shears has ever touched my hair. If it were cropped off I should be no stronger than any other man.'

This time Delilah knew that Samson had told her the truth. Swiftly she sent for the lords of the Philistines and said to them:

'Now there is no mistake. Samson has told me the secret of his strength and tonight you may take him and do to him what you will. Therefore come when darkness falls, and bring with you the eleven hundred pieces of silver, each one of you, which you promised to give me as my reward for betraying Samson.'

So they came laden with money. And that night Delilah sang to Samson more sweetly than ever before, and made love to him more delightfully. At last he fell asleep contentedly in her arms, and she signalled silently to one of the waiting Philistines, who crept into the room and cut off all Samson's hair until he was cropped like a convict.

Then she shrieked: 'Samson! Samson! The Philistines are upon you!'

At once he awoke and sprang up, shouting: 'Where are they? Let me get at them and slay them in thousands as I have done so often before!'

So saying, and not yet aware of what Delilah had done to him, Samson rushed out into the midst of his enemies—who captured him easily, bound him with cords that he could no longer break, and tore out his eyes.

Then they bound him by the foot with brass fetters and made him grind corn at the treadmill in the prison at Gaza.

... crying, 'Death to my enemies—and to me!' Samson strained forward with all his might

Full of triumph at having at last overcome and captured their most dangerous enemy, the Philistines sent to gather as many of their people as possible into Gaza to hold a festival of thanksgiving and offer a great sacrifice to their false god Dagon who, they said, had delivered Samson into their hands.

When the feast had been going for some time and the Philistines were getting drunk, they began to shout:

'Fetch Samson so that we can triumph over his weakness, and jeer and mock at our slave's blindness!'

So Samson was brought from the prison and set in a place between the two main pillars of the temple where all could see him. And the Philistines jeered and mocked and tormented him to their heart's content.

Presently, when they grew tired of their cruel sport, Samson said to the boy who was leading him:

'I am growing tired. Guide my hands to the two great pillars that support the temple so that I may lean on them.'

The boy did so, and Samson rested his hands on the two pillars while once again the Philistines mocked him—and there were over three thousand of them in the court and on the roof, including all their greatest men with their wives.

Suddenly Samson turned his blind eyes up to the heavens and cried:

'O Jahveh, true God, remember me! Give me back my strength for one moment so that I may be avenged upon the Philistines—and die with them!'

Then, in the sudden ghastly pause which followed his words, grasping one pillar in his left hand and the other in his right hand, crying, 'Death to my enemies—and to me!' he strained forward with all his might.

And, although his hair had grown only a little, Jahveh gave him back his full strength for that one moment: the pillars broke in half and the whole building came crashing down on Samson and on all the gathered host of Philistines who had been mocking him.

Not one escaped; and the people he slew at his death were more than those he had slain in his life.

THE STORY OF RUTH

In the days when the judges, who included both Jephthah and Samson, ruled over Israel, there was a famine in the land of Palestine, and a certain Israelite called Elimelech, with his wife Naomi, left Bethlehem which is near Jerusalem and went to dwell in the country of Moab on the east side of the River Jordan.

Presently Elimelech died, leaving his two grown-up sons to look after Naomi. They married women of Moab called Orpah and Ruth—and shortly afterwards died also, leaving them widows as well as their mother Naomi.

After this Naomi decided to return to Bethlehem, for she felt sure that her relations there would not let her starve—and now that her sons were dead she had no one to care for her or win her bread except her two daughters-in-law.

As to them she said: 'Return both of you to your mothers' houses, and may Jahveh bless you and deal kindly with you, as you have dealt kindly with the dead and with me. And may each of you find a new husband and bear children and make happy homes for yourselves.'

They replied: 'No, no! We will return with you to your home.'

But Naomi said: 'Think well before you do. I am old and will have no more sons for you to marry—and if I did you could hardly wait until they were old enough to be your husbands! No, think again. I am truly sorry to lose you, and am heartbroken that my sons died almost as soon as you were married to them, and that you had no children. But think of your future, and go back to your own homes as I bid you.'

Then Orpah wept and kissed Naomi goodbye, and set off for her parents' home.

But Ruth did not go.

'Why do you wait?' asked Naomi. 'You see that your sister-in-law has gone back to her people and her gods. Why do not you do the same?'

But Ruth replied: 'Do not ask me to leave you or to cease from following wherever you go; for where you go there will I go also; and where you live there will I live; your people shall be my people and your God my God. Where you die I will die also, and there shall I be buried. And may Jahveh kill me at once if I let anything but death part us.'

When Naomi saw that Ruth was in earnest she kissed and blessed her; and the two bereaved women set out together across the Jordan and up through the wilderness to the little village of Bethlehem on its hill above the fertile slopes where the corn was fast ripening to harvest.

Now it was the custom at harvest time for those who owned rich cornlands to allow people like Ruth and Naomi, who had no corn of their own, to follow after the harvesters and glean—gather up any stalks or ears of corn which had been left behind. For in the days when the harvesters cut the corn by hand with a sickle and bound into sheaves each armful when it became too much to hold, a good deal was sure to be dropped or scattered over the fields.

So it was natural for Ruth to say to Naomi: 'Let me go down to the fields, for the barley harvest is just beginning, and glean the ears of corn behind whoever will allow me to do so.'

'Go, my daughter,' said Naomi. And so Ruth went down to the cornfields and began to glean behind the harvesters who were reaping the barley that belonged to a rich man of Bethlehem named Boaz.

Later in the day Boaz came down to see how the harvest was getting on:

'Jahveh be with you!' he cried to the reapers, and they answered: 'May Jahveh bless you also.'

Presently he saw Ruth and asked: 'Whose girl is this?'

'It is the Moabite girl who came back with Naomi, Elimelech's widow, out of the land of Moab,' answered Boaz's bailiff, who was in charge of his reapers. 'She came early this morning and begged to be allowed to glean after the reapers; and she has been at it ever since with scarcely a pause.'

Then Boaz smiled at Ruth and said: 'Young woman, I am pleased that you should glean so diligently after my reapers. Continue to do so, and do not leave my fields for any others, but stay with the maidens of my own household. You will be quite safe with them, and none of the men will insult you or be a nuisance to you. And when you are thirsty after bending in the hot sun, go and help yourself from the pails of water which my men have brought from the well.'

Ruth bowed low before Boaz and said: 'Why are you so kind to me, seeing that I am a stranger and quite unknown to you?'

But Boaz answered: 'I have learned who you are, and all you have done for your mother-in-law since your husband's death, and how you have left your father and your mother and your home and your people to follow Naomi. May Jahveh bless you and reward you; the least I can do is to let you glean in my fields.'

'Now blessings on you, and on the God of Israel, that I have found favour in your sight, my lord,' said Ruth.

'When you are hungry', went on Boaz, 'come and eat with us.' And when the reapers broke off for food, he made sure that Ruth had bread and parched corn with the rest.

In fact he was so taken with her that he said privately to his men: 'Let her glean even among the sheaves which you have set up in stooks, and let her see that she may do so freely and without blame. And you might let fall a few handfuls on purpose for her to glean, without letting her realize what you are doing.'

So Ruth gleaned until it was too dark to do any more. And when she beat out the grain from the stalks which she had gleaned she found that she had nearly a bushel of barley. This was about half a normal sack of corn—almost more than she could carry.

When Ruth got home and showed her mother-in-law how much she had gleaned Naomi asked:

'Where did you glean today? Blessings on whoever let you gather the fallen ears behind his reapers!'

'The man's name was Boaz,' said Ruth.

'May Jahveh bless him!' cried Naomi. 'And indeed I see Jahveh's hand in this; for Boaz is a kinsman of mine—and only Jahveh could have led you to glean in his fields out of all others.'

'He told me to glean in his fields until the end of the harvest,' said Ruth.

'Do as he says,' advised Naomi. 'And keep with his land-girls, for that will be both safe and seemly for you.'

So Ruth went each day with the land-girls of Boaz and gleaned until the end of the barley harvest, and then until the wheat harvest was in also.

When all the corn was in Naomi said to Ruth:

'This night Boaz will be winnowing the grain on his threshing floor—blowing away the chaff with fans. Go to the winnowing, and when it is ended kneel at the feet of Boaz and ask his help for me: for my husband's lands still remain, and as my sons are dead without sons of their own, they may descend to Boaz as next of kin in the male line.'

Ruth did as Naomi told her, and Boaz promised to befriend both her and her mother-in-law. For Boaz had already fallen in love with Ruth. And when all the complicated legal business was settled, and Boaz proved the legitimate owner of the fields which had belonged to Elimelech, he married Ruth and took Naomi into their home to pass a comfortable old age.

And Boaz and Ruth lived happily all the days of their life and had a son called Obed who was the father of Jesse, the father of David the greatest of all the kings of Israel.

Book Five

DAVID, KING OF ISRAEL

SAMUEL THE PROPHET

IN THE days when the judges ruled Israel, and the Philistines were still the overlords of all Palestine, there was a woman called Hannah. She was the second of the two wives of an important Israelite called Elkanah, and, although she had no children while his other wife bore him several children, he loved her more.

Each year the whole family came down from their mountain home to nearby Shiloh (which is about twenty miles north of Jerusalem) to worship Jahveh in the temple there and celebrate his sacred festival. And because Elkanah always gave the richest portion at the feast to Hannah, his other wife always went out of her way to insult Hannah and mock her for being childless.

Then Hannah would fret, and go off her food, and Elkanah would try to comfort her.

'Why are you crying, Hannah?' he asked one year. 'Why are

you not eating? Why are you grieving like this? Cheer up! Do I not take better care of you than ten sons would?'

So Hannah ate and drank and tried to smile. But when she had the chance she went into the temple and prayed silently to Jahveh, saying:

'Let me have a son—and I will dedicate him to serve you all his life as a Nazarite with uncut hair.'

As she prayed, rocking her body from side to side and moving her lips in silent words, Eli, the high priest of Shiloh, saw her and thought she was drunk. Frowning, he strode forward and rebuked her, saying:

'How dare you come drunken into the sacred place of Jahveh?'

But Hannah answered humbly: 'I am not drunk, my lord—indeed strong drink has not passed my lips today. But I am a woman with a sorrowful heart, and am making my prayer to Jahveh to help me.'

Then Eli blessed her, saying: 'Go in peace, and may the God of Israel grant your prayers.'

So Hannah went out of the temple comforted, and ate and drank and was happy. And sure enough, before the year was out she bore a son whom she named Samuel, which means 'Asked of God'. And when he was old enough she took him to Shiloh and dedicated him to the service of Jahveh, saying to Eli, the high priest:

'I am the woman whom you accused of drunkenness and afterwards blessed. And I am blessed, for I have borne a son—this boy Samuel whom I bring to be dedicated to Jahveh according to my vow.'

After this Samuel dwelt in the temple at Shiloh, although he was only a child, and did all that Eli instructed him. He wore a white cope over the little coat which his mother made for him and brought each year when she and Elkanah came to the festival to offer sacrifice to Jahveh.

Hannah now had several other children; but she still loved Samuel best, and made sure of visiting him with his new coat every year. But to Eli the priest he was like a much loved grandson. For Eli was very old, and his own sons had turned from the worship of Jahveh and would help themselves to the sacrifices and behave wickedly with the priestesses of Ashtoreth, and Eli was in despair about them.

Samuel grew in the temple and learned to help Eli in all things relating to the worship of Jahveh. He was still only a boy, however, when one evening a strange thing befell.

Eli was nodding in his chair, and the lamp that shone before the Ark of the Covenant was burning low. Samuel was asleep; but he woke suddenly to hear a voice calling: 'Samuel! Samuel!'

'Here am I!' he answered, jumping up. And thinking Eli had called him he ran to where he was, repeating: 'Here I am! You called me!'

'I did not call you,' said Eli. 'Go back to sleep.'

So Samuel returned to bed. But almost at once the same voice called again: 'Samuel! Samuel!'

'Here I am!' cried Samuel, jumping up and running to Eli. 'This time you did call me.'

'No, I never called you, my child,' answered Eli. 'So lie down again.'

Scarcely was Samuel in bed again when the voice called a third time: 'Samuel! Samuel!'

And Samuel ran straight to Eli, exclaiming: 'This time you certainly called me, and here I am.'

Then Eli said: 'Go and lie down. And if you are called again do not get out of bed, but say: "Speak, Lord, for your servant is listening."'

So Samuel went back to bed. And sure enough the voice called yet again: 'Samuel! Samuel!'

And Samuel sat up in bed and replied: 'Here am I! Speak, Lord, for your servant is listening.'

Then the voice said: 'Samuel, you shall be the first prophet in Israel, for a prophet is one who hears the voice of Jahveh and speaks his will to the people. Now I speak to you for the first time and tell you that a terrible fate lies in store for the sons of Eli, since they have behaved wickedly and loosely, turning away from the worship of the true God to follow after idols and their evil worshippers.'

In the morning Samuel rose as usual and opened the doors of the temple. But he did not dare to tell Eli what he had heard.

However, Eli asked him, saying: 'What is it that was said to you in the night? I beg you not to hide it from me, however much it may grieve me.'

So Samuel told him all; and Eli bowed his head, saying: 'It was Jahveh who spoke: let him do what seems good to him.'

Eli never doubted that Jahveh had spoken to Samuel. And as the years passed Jahveh spoke to him many times more, until it was known throughout all Israel that Samuel of Shiloh was a true prophet of Jahveh.

But Samuel's words did not turn the majority of the people back to the worship of the true God. Indeed the time came when they felt that they could fend for themselves without help or blessing, and they decided to make war against the Philistines and drive them out of all the lands which their ancestors had taken in Joshua's day.

So they fought a pitched battle and were defeated with the loss of about four thousand men. Then, fearing greatly what might happen to them, they turned back to Jahveh, crying:

'Why has our God smitten us like this? Let us fetch the Ark of the Covenant from Shiloh and carry it into battle. Then Jahveh will fight for us and scatter the Philistines as he scattered the hosts of Pharaoh in the days of Moses.'

So they sent to Shiloh; and the two sons of Eli took up the Ark of the Covenant, setting on their shoulders the poles which passed through the rings at its corners, and carried it to where the army of Israel was encamped. And the Israelites greeted it with such a shout of joy that it echoed back from the mountains round about them.

The Philistines heard the noise of the shout and said: 'What is the meaning of this great noise which these Hebrews are making?'

When they heard about the Ark of the Covenant some cried: 'Now the god of these Hebrews will destroy us as he destroyed the Egyptians when they crossed over the Red Sea!' (The Philistines called the Israelites 'Hebrews', which in their language meant 'Those who have crossed over', since they had crossed first over the Red Sea and then over the Jordan into their country.)

But the rest cried: 'Let us show that we are free men and no slaves to this gang of invaders who have tried to conquer and colonize our country!'

So they all rushed into battle and fought so well that they defeated the Israelites with great slaughter, killing thirty thousand foot soldiers alone. And the Ark of the Covenant was captured by them, and Eli's two sons who carried it were killed.

Then a messenger came running from the battlefield to Shiloh, with his clothes torn and dust on his head. And when he told the news all in the city cried out and mourned.

Then he came to where Eli sat by the gate of the temple, and Eli said: 'What is the meaning of all this noise and tumult in the city?'

'Israel is defeated by the Philistines!' gasped the messenger, 'and thousands have been slaughtered! Your two sons are among the dead, and the Ark of the Covenant has been captured by the Philistines.'

When he heard this Eli fell backwards off his seat. And the fall broke his neck, for he was by now an old man of ninety-eight, and he had grown fat and heavy with age.

But the Philistines carried off the Ark in triumph to their city of Ashdod and put it in the temple of their god Dagon, in front of his statue.

Next day, when the priest went to open the temple, they found that the statue of Dagon had fallen on its face in front of the Ark of the Covenant of Jahveh. They set it up again quickly before any of his worshippers should see what had happened. But next morning the statue lay as before—and this time its head and hands were broken off. Moreover the people of Ashdod and the country near by were suddenly smitten with bleeding piles and other painful diseases, and this they put down to the vengeance of Jahveh for the insults offered to the Ark of the Covenant.

So the people of Ashdod gathered together and said to the lords of the Philistines who ruled the city: 'Take away the Ark of Jahveh before a worse thing happens to us."

But when the Ark was taken to the Philistine city of Gath, all the people there developed bleeding piles also. And the same thing happened when it was carried to Ekron; and the people of Ekron cried, 'Take back this deadly reliquary of the Israelites before it does more damage to us'; for after it had remained some months in Ekron many people began to die of painful diseases in their intestines, while all the rest suffered exceedingly from the bleeding piles.

Thoroughly frightened, the Philistines set the Ark on a cart and sent it back to the Israelites with presents of jewels and a special offering of five golden mice—since the Philistines, like the Greeks, believed that mice carried diseases and pestilences.

The first Israelites who received back the Ark looked inside it, and were struck blind; but afterwards they were more careful and took it for safe keeping to a hill a few miles north of Jerusalem where the priests hid it and guarded it for twenty years.

At the end of that time Samuel called for a holy war against the Philistines. But first he gathered the people of Israel together and preached to them, saying:

'If you return whole-heartedly to the service of Jahveh, and turn away entirely from the false gods of the Philistines such as Ashtoreth and Dagon, Jahveh will help you to win the war against the Philistines and set Israel free from them.'

Soon the people of Israel were converted from their evil idolatry. They broke the images of Baal and Ashtoreth and Dagon, cut down the sacred groves, killed or banished the evil priests and priestesses who had conducted the moonlight ceremonies to these gods, and returned to the worship of the one God, Jahveh.

When the Philistines heard that the Israelites were gathered together at Mizpah, they called out their army and sent a vast host against them. And the Israelites said to Samuel:

'We are very much afraid that the Philistines may defeat us.

But pray and sacrifice to Jahveh without stopping, and we will go forward believing that he will save us from them and give victory to his Chosen People.'

So Samuel prayed and offered up burnt sacrifices for dear life and a great battle took place during which, when victory hung in the balance, a tremendous thunderstorm broke over the Philistines, but not over the Israelites, which so terrified the Philistines that they turned and fled while the Israelites pursued them slaying and slaying until they were too tired to go farther.

The victory was so complete that all the land of Israel was free from the Philistines for a whole generation. During all that time Samuel ruled as judge over Israel, and went on circuit from year to year throughout the land until he grew old.

Then he made his sons judges over Israel: but they were quite unworthy of him—taking bribes and giving false judgments.

So the people of Israel sent their representatives to Samuel, saying: 'You are old and your sons are corrupt. Therefore, great prophet, give us a king like all the other nations round about us.'

At first Samuel tried to persuade them against having a king, telling them how much of their freedom they would lose, and how a king would tax them and load his favourites with gifts, and might in the end become a tyrant.

But they were obstinate and continued to insist: 'All the neighbouring nations have kings: we do not want to be different. Give us a king.'

'A king you shall have,' said Samuel at length. 'Jahveh will show me who it is to be. Now return each of you to his own city and wait.'

Samuel prayed and waited. Presently the word of Jahveh came to him: 'Tomorrow I will send a man of the tribe of Benjamin. Anoint him king, for I have chosen him to save my people from the Philistines.'

Next day, as he was leaving his house to go to a great feast at the temple, there came a fine tall young man with one servant who said to him:

'Tell me, I beg of you, where may I find the prophet Samuel?'

'I am Samuel the prophet,' was the answer, 'and I know all about you, for Jahveh puts it into my heart. You are Saul, the son of Kish, and you are seeking for your father's asses which have strayed away and are lost. Forget about them, for they are found and tomorrow you must hasten home—for your father has given up worrying about his asses and is worrying about you, lest you have come to any harm. But in seeking asses you have found a kingdom; for Jahveh has commanded me to anoint you with the holy oil—and in due time you will be chosen first king of Israel, and will do much to free Israel from the yoke of the Philistines.'

Then Samuel led the dazed Saul to the feast and served him with the best portion. Afterwards he took him back to his house and anointed him and told him more of the will of Jahveh.

Next day Saul returned home, saying nothing about all that had happened to him. But from the moment of his anointing he was changed: for Jahveh had given him greater strength and wisdom, and also the power of prophecy—so much so that those who met him marvelled, exclaiming: 'Is Saul also among the prophets?'

Samuel, however, called a great assembly of the Israelites to Mizpah. When they were all gathered Samuel cast lots—and the lot fell upon the tribe of Benjamin. Again he cast, and the lot fell upon Kish's family. A third time he cast, and the lot fell upon Saul.

Saul knew what was coming, and for a moment he was afraid and hid. But Samuel saw by his power where he was hidden, and Saul was brought out before all the people—and he was a head taller than any of them.

Then Samuel cried: 'Behold the man whom Jahveh has chosen to rule over you!'

And the people of Israel shouted all together: 'God save the king!'

So Saul took command of Israel and led the army to war, and for sixteen years waged war against the Philistines, defeating them in several battles and driving them back until they ceased to trouble Israel.

Then Samuel said to him: 'The word of Jahveh has come true. Set out and make war upon the Amalekites, and destroy their city of Amalek utterly, sparing none nor taking any booty.'

Saul did as he was bidden, and the Israelites drove the Amalekites almost to the borders of Egypt and captured the city of Amalek and seized Agag, the king of it. But then Saul disobeyed the commands of Jahveh, for he not only kept Agag alive but also the best of the sheep and oxen and the choice spoils of the stricken city.

When Samuel knew of this he knew that Jahveh would no longer be with Saul nor inspire him, and he was much grieved. He rose early in the morning and went to meet Saul who was returning in triumph from Amalek and had reached Gilgal in the Jordan Valley near where Jericho had stood, the place where Joshua had set up the twelve stones from the bed of the river.

'Blessed be you, prophet of Israel,' said Saul when Samuel came before him. 'You see that I have done what Jahveh commanded and conquered the Amalekites.'

'What is the meaning of the bleating of sheep which reaches my ears?' asked Samuel severely. 'And why do I hear the lowing of oxen?'

'We brought them from the lands of the Amalekites,' answered Saul, 'for the people spared the best of the sheep and oxen—to sacrifice to Jahveh. The rest we have utterly destroyed.'

'Wait a little and hear what Jahveh has taught me only last night,' said Samuel. 'When you were of no importance—an unknown youth among the smallest of the tribes of Israel—did not Jahveh choose you to be king of all Israel? And did he not send you, giving his commands through my lips, to destroy the Amalekites absolutely and to burn Amalek and everything in it? Why did you not obey the commands of Jahveh, but have brought with you a prisoner and the choicest spoils?'

'I have obeyed Jahveh in all things,' said Saul. 'I have conquered and destroyed the Amalekites and brought Agag, their king, as my captive. If the people have kept some few of the sheep and oxen, it is only to sacrifice them to Jahveh here in this holy place of Gilgal.'

Then Samuel drew himself up and cried: 'Do not think that you can deceive Jahveh! To obey is better than any number of sacrifices, and rebellion is as the sin of witchcraft and setting your own will before Jahveh's is a form of idolatry. Because you have rejected and disobeyed the word of Jahveh, he has rejected you, and you are no longer king of Israel.'

'I have sinned—I admit it!' cried Saul. 'But I only did it because I was afraid that the people would rebel against me if I did not let them have some of the spoils of the Amalekites. Pardon me, I beg of you, and set me right with Jahveh.'

But Samuel took hold of Saul's robe and tore it across, saying: 'Even as I rend this garment, so has Jahveh rent the kingdom from you this day and has given it to another who is better than you are.'

'Do not shame me before my people,' begged Saul, 'but lead us in worship of Jahveh.' So Samuel did as Saul requested. But then he said: 'Bring Agag, the king of the Amalekites, before me.'

Then Agag was brought, and came before Samuel, walking delicately. And Samuel said:

'Even as you have made women childless, so shall your mother be childless among women this day.'

And he took a sword and chopped Agag into pieces there and then.

After this Samuel returned home, while Saul went back to his own palace. But Samuel never again came to visit Saul, though he mourned for him, and was sorry that Jahveh had cast him out.

THE BOY DAVID

AFTER Saul had forfeited his right to be the divinely inspired king of Israel by disobeying Jahveh's commands, Samuel the prophet continued to mourn for him.

But at length the message of Jahveh came to him: 'Samuel, cease from mourning over Saul's loss, since I have rejected him. But fill your horn with oil and go to the house of Jesse, the grandson of Ruth and Boaz, in Bethlehem, for I have chosen a king for Israel from among his eight sons.'

'How can I go?' asked Samuel. 'If Saul hears of it he will kill me.'

'Take a heifer with you and say that you come to sacrifice to Jahveh; and call Jesse to the sacrifice, and after it return to his house and there I will show you which of his sons is the chosen king. For I look into the hearts of men, not upon their outward appearance, and I will show you which he is.'

So Samuel did as Jahveh had bidden him and came to Bethlehem, bringing the heifer with him for sacrifice. The elders of the town trembled at his coming, and asked:

'Do you come in peace?'

'I come in peace,' answered Samuel. 'I come to sacrifice to Jahveh. Therefore make yourselves clean and join me at the sacrifice.'

When this was over Samuel went to spend the night at Jesse's house and told him that Jahveh had sent him to choose one of his sons to fulfil a very high mission in Israel. So Jesse sent them to him one by one: Eliab, the eldest, first, and then the rest in turn until seven had appeared—and seven had been refused, for Jahveh gave Samuel no sign that the future king stood before him.

Then said Samuel to Jesse: 'Jahveh has not chosen any of these. Are all your children here?'

'I have one other son,' answered Jesse, 'but he is only a boy and he is out tending the sheep.'

'Send for him and let him come to me,' said Samuel, 'for we may not sit down to supper until I have seen him.'

So they sent for the youngest son, and presently the boy David came and stood before Samuel, a handsome boy with a ruddy complexion and beautiful clear-cut features.

At once Jahveh spoke in Samuel's heart, saying: 'Rise and anoint him, for this is he.'

So Samuel took his horn of oil and poured it on his head. And the spirit of Jahveh was with David from that day on, and from time to time would take control of him suddenly, giving him strength and wisdom far beyond his years.

Meanwhile the Philistines were overrunning Israel again, and on their march towards Jerusalem and Gilgal they stopped to gather together all their armies at a place called Socoh only ten miles from Jerusalem.

Saul and his armies came out to meet them and camped in the Vale of Elah, which runs for most of the thirteen miles between Socoh and Bethlehem. The Philistines were encamped on the mountain on one side and the Israelites on the mountain on the other side, with the valley between them.

And there went out a champion from the camp of the Philistines named Goliath of Gath, a huge man over nine feet tall. He wore a bronze helmet on his head and was clothed in a coat of mail weighing a hundredweight and a half. He had bronze greaves on his legs and a bronze gorget, and the shaft of his spear was like a weaver's beam, while the iron head of it weighed nearly twenty-eight pounds.

Goliath stood on the hillside and shouted to the warriors of Israel: 'Why are you setting your armies in battle array? Am I not a Philistine and you the servants of Saul? Choose a man to represent you and let him come down and fight me. If he kills me we will be your servants, and if I kill him you shall serve us. I defy the armies of Israel: show me a *man* and we will fight together!'

But when Saul and the Israelites saw and heard Goliath they were afraid; and none of them dared accept his challenge.

Now Jesse's three eldest sons were serving in Saul's army, and it chanced that one day Jesse said to David: 'Take a bushel of parched corn and ten loaves to your brothers in the camp; and take also ten cheeses as a present to the colonel in whose regiment they are serving. Then come back and tell me how your brothers are.'

So David got up early in the morning, slung the half-sack of corn over his shoulder, put the loaves of bread and the little ewes'-milk cheeses in a basket and set off down the Vale of Elah, having first found someone to look after the sheep while he was away.

When David reached Socoh he found the two armies lined up on either side of the valley as if about to begin a battle. So he left his sack and basket with one of the camp guards and hastened through the lines until he found his brothers.

While he was talking with them Goliath of Gath came out of the Philistine lines, down into the valley, and challenged the Israelites to send a champion against him, as he had done every day for the last forty days.

But, as usual, the Israelites drew back afraid and not one of them dared to accept Goliath's challenge.

When David saw and heard Goliath he asked: 'What reward is offered to the man who kills this big Philistine and restores Israel's reputation for valour? Someone ought to go and slay this insolent boaster.'

'Whoever kills Goliath will receive a great reward from King Saul,' was the answer. 'Not only a large sum in gold, but also one of the king's daughters to be his wife, and freedom from taxation for his whole family.'

When Eliab, his eldest brother, heard David's words, he said to him angrily: 'What are you doing here, instead of looking after the sheep at home? I suppose you have sneaked off to see the battle? You should stick to matters you know something about, and not come here making foolish remarks about the conduct of the war. I know the sort of proud and empty things you have got into the way of saying lately.'

But David repeated his question about why no one went to fight Goliath, and at last Saul heard about it and sent for David.

When he was brought before the king and rebuked for his words David said: 'There is nothing to be afraid of. I will go and fight this Philistine if no one else dares.'

'You!' exclaimed Saul. 'What could you do against him? You are only a boy, and he has been a warrior skilled in arms for many years.'

'Well,' said David, 'twice while I have been looking after my father's sheep the flock has been attacked by wild animals. The first time it was a lion, and the second time it was a bear. Each of them carried off a lamb from the flock, but on both occasions I went after the creature, saved the lamb and killed first the lion and then the bear. And I don't see why I should not be able to do the same to this great hulking Philistine who has defied the armies of Jahveh. For Jahveh saved me from the claws and teeth of both lion and bear, and he will preserve me from the hand of this Philistine in the same way.'

Saul was convinced by what David had said, and replied: 'Very well, go and fight Goliath—and may Jahveh help you.'

Moreover he lent David his armour and sword. But when his squires girded them on to him, David found that they were so heavy that he could not move, and he exclaimed:

'I cannot go in these pieces of armour—help me to take them off again!'

So, just as he was, in his shepherd's tunic, with a staff in his hand and a pouch at his belt through which was stuck his sling, David set out to fight Goliath of Gath. But first he went down to the stream in the valley and chose five stones worn smooth by the water, and put them in his pouch.

Then he took his sling in his hand and went towards the Philistine giant. Goliath came on, with his shield-bearer beside him, and when he saw David he roared with laughter; for David was only a boy still, tanned by the sun and bonny of countenance.

The giant roared at David: 'Do you take me for a dog that you come against me with a stick?' And he cursed David by all the gods of the Philistines, and shouted: 'Come within my reach, and I will tear you in pieces and give your flesh to the fowls of the air and the beasts of the field.'

Then said David to the huge Philistine: 'You come against me with a sword and a spear and a shield. But I come against you in the name of Jahveh, the God of the people of Israel whom you have defied. This day he will deliver you into my hand, and I will fell you and cut off your head and give the bodies of you and many of the Philistines to the vultures and wild beasts so that all the world may know that Israel worships the true God. And everyone gathered here shall know that Jahveh saves by other means than with sword and spear: for the battle will end as he wishes—and this time he will give you into our hands.'

At this Goliath rushed forward, mad with rage, roaring like a lion and waving his sword over his head to cut David into pieces.

But David put his hand into his pouch and took out one of the smooth stones. Quietly he fitted it into the pouch of his sling, and as Goliath drew near he waved the sling round and round his head and then let the end go. Straight as an arrow flew the stone and struck Goliath on his forehead—so hard that the stone sank into his head.

Down fell Goliath with a crash on to his face and lay still. Then David darted forward, drew Goliath's sword—for he had none of his own—and hacked off his head with it.

When the Philistines saw their champion fall they turned and fled. And the Israelites rushed after them, shouting in triumph, and pursued them out of the valley into the plain, and across it right to the gates of Ekron and the nearby city of Gath. And in that rout they slew thousands.

When Saul saw David go out to fight Goliath he said to Abner, his general: 'Whose son is that youth?'

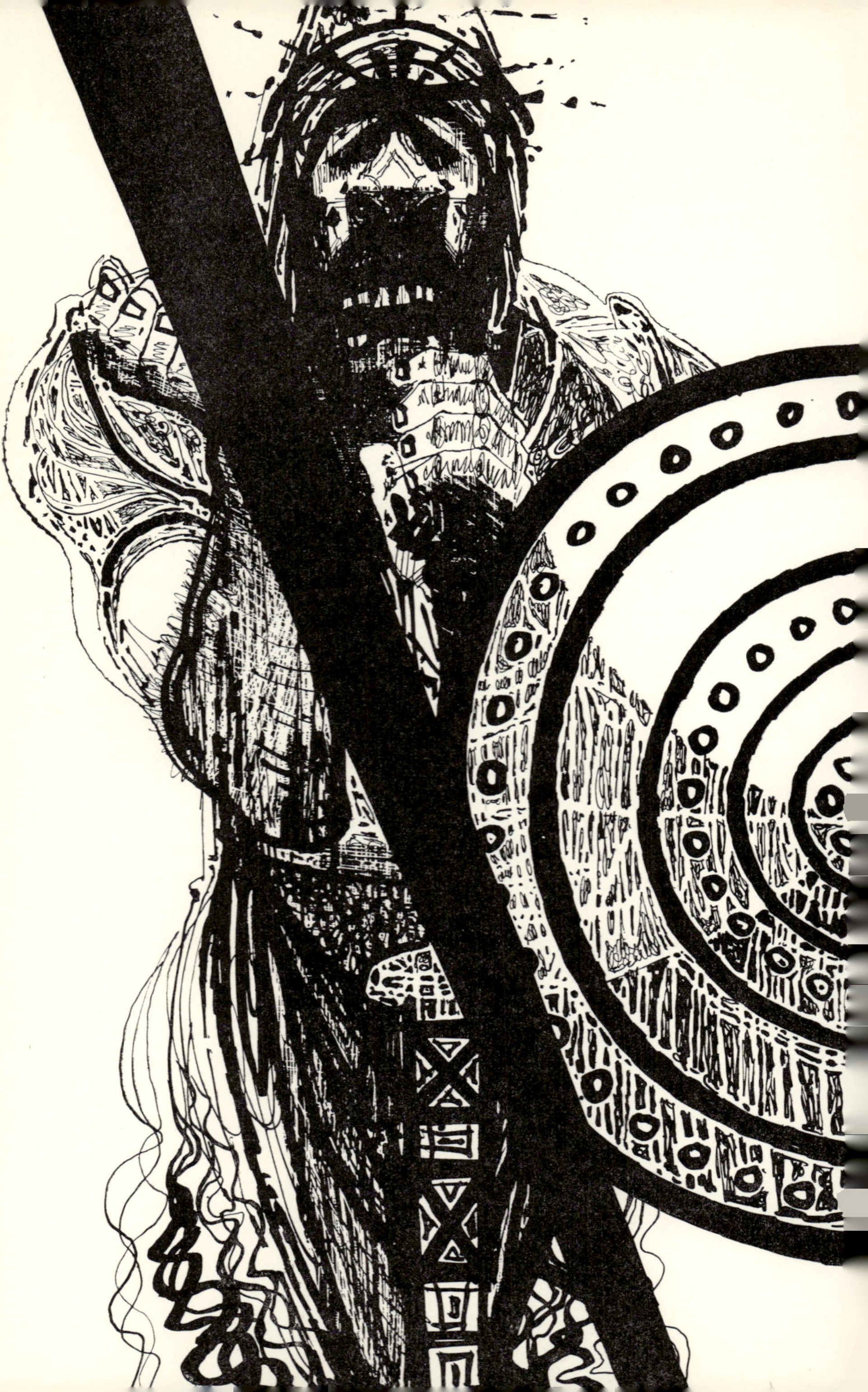

And Abner answered: 'O King, live for ever, I do not know.'

'Find out whose son this boy is,' commanded Saul, 'and bring him to me.'

So when David returned from killing the giant Philistine, Abner took him and brought him to Saul with Goliath's head still in his hand. And Saul said to him:

'Whose son are you, young man?'

'I am the son of your servant Jesse of Bethlehem,' answered David.

When David's audience with Saul was ended he met Saul's son Jonathan, and the two boys became friends on the instant. And David remained in the camp with his new friend Jonathan, and very soon became Saul's personal attendant. For since the spirit of Jahveh had left him, Saul was troubled from time to time by fits of melancholy madness as if an evil spirit had entered into him. His attendants decided that the best cure for these fits was to find someone skilled in playing the harp who would always be at hand to soothe Saul with music. And it turned out that David had this skill, and whenever the fit seized Saul, David would be fetched from Jonathan's quarters and would play sweetly on the harp until Saul was refreshed and well and the evil spirit left him for the time being.

As David grew from a boy into a handsome young man, Saul gave him a high command in his army, and David would lead his regiment to battle and return victorious; for Jahveh was with him and made all that he did prosper.

But it chanced one day, as the army returned to Jerusalem from a great battle in which a record number of Philistines had been slaughtered, that the women of Israel came out of the city to welcome them, dancing as they played their tambourines and three-stringed instruments called 'shalishim', and singing triumphantly:

'Saul has slain his thousands and David his ten thousands!'

When he heard these words Saul was furiously angry, and exclaimed: 'They credit David with slaying ten thousands, and me only with thousands! They'll be giving him my kingdom next!'

Goliath rushed forward, mad with rage

And from that day he began to look at David with jealousy and suspicion. And next time the evil spirit entered into him and he was seized with one of his fits, while David was playing the harp to soothe him Saul snatched up a javelin and flung it at David, exclaiming: 'I'll pin you to the wall with this!'

Twice he tried to kill David with the javelin; and twice David avoided it and fled away from Saul in time. And Saul was afraid, for he began to realize that Jahveh was with David and protected him. So he made David the colonel of a regiment and sent him on expeditions far away from Jerusalem, where the royal palace now was, hoping he would be killed by the Philistines.

But David returned victorious each time, and the people loved him more and more for his easy, open ways, and for mingling with them freely as he did. And Saul grew more and more jealous and afraid.

However, he hid his jealousy, and pretended to treat David as a son, and said to him:

'I will give you one of my daughters to be your wife. Jonathan tells me that you and Michal love each other: you shall marry her. But as a dowry you must bring me trophies to show that you have killed two hundred Philistines.'

Saul said this hoping that David would be killed while procuring this dowry. But David and his men set an ambush and slew two hundred Philistines and the dowry was paid easily.

Saul feared to refuse his daughter to David after this, and he also thought: 'Perhaps I can persuade Michal to betray David to the Philistines, just as Delilah betrayed Samson.'

After the wedding, however, Saul was unable to restrain his hatred and fear. So he commanded his son Jonathan and all his servants to go and slay David immediately.

But Jonathan warned David, saying: 'My father has sent me to kill you, and his servants are on their way to make sure that you are dead. Therefore hide at once in a secret place where no one can find you, and tomorrow I will plead with him and tell you what success I have in making peace between you.'

So David hid, and the slayers could not find him. But next day Jonathan spoke boldly to his father and said:

'To kill David would be a grievous sin, the worst kind of murder. For he has done nothing to deserve death, nor plotted against you in any way. Indeed he not only killed Goliath, but scattered and defeated the Philistines and has led your armies to victory again and again. To shed his innocent blood would bring the vengeance of Jahveh not only upon you, but on the people of Israel as well.'

Saul took note of what Jonathan said, and realized its truth, and swore a great oath:

'Before Jahveh, and calling down his vengeance on me if I break my oath, I swear that not only shall David not be slain, but I will protect and advance him and love him no less than I love you, Jonathan my son.'

So Jonathan brought David into Saul's presence, and Saul embraced him, asking his forgiveness and calling him his son.

But next time the Philistines attacked Israel, and David went out and defeated them with a great slaughter, Saul's jealousy flared up again. The evil spirit entered into him, and as David sat with him Saul suddenly snatched up a javelin and tried to pin him to the wall with it.

David, however, avoided the murderous stroke and escaped out of the palace and sought shelter in his own house. He knew that he would be followed and slaughtered there, nevertheless, and so he got Michal, his wife, to let him down out of a window on the end of a rope.

When he had gone she arranged a pillow and a bolster in the bed to look like David, and said to Saul's messengers:

'My husband is ill. Look, there he lies in bed. Be quiet and do not wake him.'

The messengers reported this to Saul, who commanded them to return and bring the bed with David in it so that he could transfix him that very night with a javelin.

When Saul found how he had been cheated of his vengeance, he was furious with Michal for letting David go. But she said:

'He told me to let him down out of the window, and threatened to kill me if I did not obey him.'

And Saul believed what she said and did not punish her.

David, however, escaped from Jerusalem and went to Ramah where Samuel was, and told him all that Saul had done and tried to do to him.

Presently Saul arrived at Ramah with an army to kill David. But Samuel told him straightly that David had been chosen by Jahveh to be the next king of Israel. And a fit of madness seized Saul, causing him to tear off his clothes and roll naked on the ground.

And when he came to his senses again David had fled from Ramah and sought the help of Jonathan, his devoted friend.

THE WITCH OF EN-DOR

WHEN David escaped from Saul there was like to be civil war in Israel, for many sided with him, while others remained faithful to the king.

At first Jonathan, Saul's eldest son but David's closest friend, tried yet again to heal the breach and make the present king and the king-to-be friends again. But when Saul tried to kill him also with a javelin, Jonathan realized that it was hopeless. So he went and warned David that there was no hope of a reconciliation, and bade him go as far away from Jerusalem as possible.

And he said: 'Go in peace. I will raise no hand against you, remembering our true friendship. But I cannot go with you, for I must remain loyal to my father.'

So David escaped from Jerusalem and out of Israel; and at first he was in deadly peril, being forced to seek shelter among the Philistines in Gath. Here he was nearly recognized and put to death, but escaped by pretending to be mad—scrabbling on the doors and dribbling at the mouth.

Later he hid in the cave of Adullam in the mountain between Mizpah and Socoh; and here many of Saul's followers deserted and came to join him.

Saul came out with an army to kill David and punish the rebels; but David managed to avoid a pitched battle with him, though he was only saved by a sudden incursion of the Philistines against whom Saul was forced to turn and fight.

After the battle Saul continued in pursuit of David, and camped one night in the wilderness of En-Gedi where the cave of Adullam was. And David crept into the camp during the night and cut off the lower part of Saul's coat without waking him.

In the morning David came before Saul at the head of his well-armed band of followers, and showed him the piece he had cut off from the king's robe, saying:

'My lord King, why do you seek to slay me, seeing that I am your faithful subject and never have tried to harm you nor ever will? See, I came and stood beside you as you slept, and I held a sharp sword in my hand. How easily I could have killed you—but instead I merely cut away the hem of your garment to prove how innocent I am of any wish to harm you or raise my hand against the Lord's anointed.'

Then Saul wept and said: 'You are more righteous than I, for you have rewarded me with good whereas I have rewarded you with evil. Now I know truly that one day you will be King of Israel. But while I live let us dwell in peace, and raise no hand against each other. And swear to me before Jahveh that when I am dead and you are king, you will not deal harshly with my family or try to blot them out altogether.'

David swore this oath gladly, thinking of Jonathan, his friend. And after this Saul returned to Jerusalem, while David continued to dwell on the mountain.

Not long after this Samuel the Prophet died, and there was great mourning throughout all Israel.

None mourned him more than Saul, for now he had no means of learning the will of Jahveh nor of seeing anything of the future, since only an evil spirit came to him. And when he questioned witches and wizards they could tell him only of such ill to come that in a rage he banished them all from the land of Israel under pain of death.

Yet soon he had more need than ever to know the future, for once again he broke his oath and tried to murder David. And though once again David had Saul in his power and spared him he said to himself:

'Sooner or later Saul will succeed in killing me. I must escape right out of Israel, even if I have to go and live with the Philistines.'

So he and the six hundred men who were faithful to him went

and took service with Achish, the king of Gath. There he remained for over a year, during which time he led a force against the Amalekites, who were enemies of the Philistines as well as of the Israelites, and utterly defeated them, slaying man, woman and child until they were no more a nation.

When he returned it was to find that the hosts of the Philistines were being gathered together for a great war against Israel, and that Achish had been summoned to take part in it with his army.

Meanwhile Saul heard of the great invasion that was being prepared, and when he learned of the vast numbers that the Philistines were gathering, and that David was leading the forces of King Achish of Gath, he was in despair.

Then indeed he needed the advice and help of Samuel and lamented that there was now no prophet in Israel. He himself tried to pierce the veil of darkness, but could learn nothing either by dreams, or by pyromancy, or by clairvoyance.

Then he said to his servants: 'Find a woman who has a familiar spirit so that I may go to her to ask of the future.'

And after some search they returned, saying: 'There is a witch at En-dor who has a familiar spirit.'

So Saul disguised himself, put on mean garments, and journeyed with only two servants over the sixty miles of mountainous country from Jerusalem to En-dor, near Mount Tabor in the north of Palestine.

They came by night to the place where the witch dwelt, and Saul said to her:

'I have heard that you are greatly skilled in necromancy and can raise the dead by the power of your familiar spirit. Now, I beg you, call up from the dead whatever man I may choose.'

But the witch answered: 'You know well what King Saul has done—how he has killed or banished all witches and wizards who have familiar spirits. Why do you try to trap me like that, to bring me to my death?'

Then Saul swore her a solemn oath, saying: 'I swear by Jahveh himself that no punishment shall happen to you, but only a great reward.'

'Whom shall I call up from the dead for you?' asked the witch.
'Bring me up the prophet Samuel,' answered Saul.

The witch sank into a trance. But when her familiar spirit began its necromancy, she cried out in terror: 'Why have you deceived me? You yourself are Saul the King!'

'Do not be afraid, you are safe from me,' answered Saul. 'But tell me what you saw.'

'I saw spirits ascending out of the earth,' replied the witch, 'and they led him with whom you wish to speak.'

'What was he like?' asked Saul.

'An old man wrapped in a mantle,' she answered; and as she spoke the spirit of Samuel rose out of the earth, and Saul knew him and fell on his face before him.

'Why have you troubled me and brought me back to earth?' came the ghostly voice of the dead prophet.

'I am in great trouble,' answered Saul. 'The Philistines make war against me, and David is with my enemies. Moreover Jahveh no longer answers my prayers, either by dreams or prophecies—so I have called you to me to tell me what I should do.'

'Why do you ask, seeing that Jahveh has departed from you and has become your enemy?' asked the ghost of Samuel. 'Jahveh has done what he bade me prophesy to you while I was yet alive: he has torn the kingdom of Israel out of your hands and given it to another—to David. It was because you disobeyed the commands of Jahveh that he has done this to you—and tomorrow he will deliver you into the hands of the Philistines, and by the evening you and your sons shall be with me and even as I am.'

When he heard these terrible words Saul sank fainting to the ground; and when his senses returned to him the ghost of Samuel had departed to its own place, and the witch of En-dor was striving to revive him with food and wine.

Next day the two armies met at Aphek in the valley of Jezreel a few miles south-west of En-dor. But David was not with the Philistines. He had started out with the army of King Achish, but the other Philistines leaders had objected, saying:

'Even if he has been fighting for us, it is not safe to let him come into this battle, for he may suddenly turn against us and go over to his own people of Israel.'

So David and his own six hundred men were sent against a remnant of the Amalekites at some distance from the scene of the action. But the great host of the Philistines moved down upon Saul and his army, and very soon the Israelites broke and fled, leaving many dead in the valley of Jezreel and on the slopes of Mount Gilboa.

Saul fled with his bodyguard and the few who remained with him. But the Philistines pursued hotly and mowed many down with their arrows, including Jonathan and Saul's other sons.

At last, wounded with arrows, Saul could go no farther, and he said to his armour-bearers: 'Draw your sword and kill me before the Philistines come and torture and mock me. For there is no escape.'

But the armour-bearer would not do so, for he was too afraid.

Then Saul drew his own sword and fell upon it and so died. And his armour-bearer, seeing his beloved master dead, fell upon his sword also and died with him. After this the Philistines arrived, and finding Saul dead they cut off his head and stripped off his armour, and carried them as trophies to the cities of Philistia, and nailed them up in the temple of Ashtoreth.

But in the night such Israelites as dwelt near by came secretly and took the bodies of Saul and his sons out of the temple and buried them beyond the Jordan in Gilead.

The Philistines were not victorious for long, however. For David came up from the south like a whirlwind, and the Israelites gathered to him from every side; and wherever he led them he brought them victory.

In time the Philistines were driven out, and all the land of Israel was set free. David became king indeed—the greatest king that Israel was ever to know, though his son Solomon was the wisest and the richest.

David made his capital at Jerusalem, and built a strong wall round about the city, and began to build the great temple of Jahveh which Solomon was to complete. With him began the period of Israel's greatest power and glory. And although they had much to suffer, and were to be conquered more than once, the Israelites never again departed to any serious extent from the worship of one God, nor forfeited their claim to be his Chosen People until their mission was accomplished ten centuries later when Jesus Christ was born from among the descendants of David, King of Israel.

Titles in this Series of Illustrated Classics

CHILDREN'S ILLUSTRATED CLASSICS

(Illustrated Classics for Older Readers are listed on fourth page)

Andrew Lang's **ADVENTURES OF ODYSSEUS.** Illustrated by KIDDELL-MONROE.
The wanderings of the great Greek hero on his way home to Ithaca.

AESOP'S FABLES. Illustrated by KIDDELL-MONROE.
A definitive translation by John Warrington.

Lewis Carroll's **ALICE'S ADVENTURES IN WONDERLAND and THROUGH THE LOOKING-GLASS.** Illustrated by JOHN TENNIEL.
Here is the complete story of Alice in both topsyturvy regions.

George MacDonald's **AT THE BACK OF THE NORTH WIND.** Illustrated by E. H. SHEPARD.
This is the lovable and much loved story of Diamond.

Robert Louis Stevenson's **THE BLACK ARROW.** Illustrated by LIONEL EDWARDS.
The period is the England of the Wars of the Roses.

Anna Sewell's **BLACK BEAUTY.** Illustrated by LUCY KEMP-WELCH.

Roger Lancelyn Green's **A BOOK OF MYTHS.** Illustrated by KIDDELL-MONROE.
A retelling of the world's greatest legends and folk-tales.

THE BOOK OF NONSENSE. Edited by ROGER LANCELYN GREEN. Illustrated by CHARLES FOLKARD in colour, and with original drawings by TENNIEL, LEAR, FURNISS, HOLIDAY, HUGHES, SHEPARD and others.
Examples of 'nonsense' from ancient to modern times.

THE BOOK OF VERSE FOR CHILDREN. Collected by ROGER LANCELYN GREEN. Illustrated with two-colour drawings in the text by MARY SHILLABEER. (Not available in the U.S.A. in this edition.)

Mrs Ewing's **THE BROWNIES AND OTHER STORIES.** Illustrated by E. H. SHEPARD.
The author wrote the famous story of *The Brownies* when only twenty-three.

Mrs Molesworth's **THE CARVED LIONS.** Illustrated by LEWIS HART.
An evocative story of the Manchester of a century ago.

Captain Marryat's **THE CHILDREN OF THE NEW FOREST.** Illustrated by LIONEL EDWARDS.
A story of adventure in a wild and romantic corner of England.

Robert Louis Stevenson's **A CHILD'S GARDEN OF VERSES.** Illustrated by MARY SHILLABEER.
This collection contains a number of poems not found in other editions.

Charles Dickens's **A CHRISTMAS CAROL and THE CRICKET ON THE HEARTH.** Illustrated by C. E. BROCK.

R. M. Ballantyne's **THE CORAL ISLAND.** Illustrated by LEO BATES.
Ballantyne's most famous boys' book is illustrated with such realism that the most fascinating of islands in boys' fiction is more vivid than ever.

Mrs Molesworth's THE CUCKOO CLOCK. Illustrated by E. H. SHEPARD.
Shepard's exquisite and delicate drawings enhance the enthralling text.

E. Nesbit's THE ENCHANTED CASTLE. Illustrated by CECIL LESLIE.
A sunny garden leads to a never-never land of enchantment.

FAIRY TALES FROM THE ARABIAN NIGHTS. Illustrated by KIDDELL-MONROE.
Here are the favourite tales—the fairy tales—out of the many told in the 'Thousand and One Nights'.

FAIRY TALES OF LONG AGO. Edited by M. C. CAREY. Illustrated by D. J. WATKINS-PITCHFORD.
This varied collection takes in translations from Charles Perrault, Madame de Beaumont, the Countess d'Aulnoy of France, Asbjörnsen and Moe, etc.

Selma Lagerlöf's THE FURTHER ADVENTURES OF NILS. Illustrated by HANS BAUMHAUER.
Nils's adventures continue with his flight over lake, hill, ice, snow, forest and moor of Sweden. The artist ably interprets the visual contrasts of the journey. (Not available in the U.S.A. in this edition.) *See also* THE WONDERFUL ADVENTURES OF NILS (on third page).

Louisa M. Alcott's GOOD WIVES. Illustrated by S. VAN ABBÉ.

Frances Browne's GRANNY'S WONDERFUL CHAIR. Illustrated by DENYS WATKINS-PITCHFORD.
The author, blind from birth, draws upon the Irish fairy-stories of her childhood to add magic and colour to the whole of this enchanting book.

GRIMMS' FAIRY TALES. Illustrated by CHARLES FOLKARD.

HANS ANDERSEN'S FAIRY TALES. Illustrated by HANS BAUMHAUER.
A new English rendering, including some new and outstanding tales.

Mary Mapes Dodge's HANS BRINKER. Illustrated by HANS BAUMHAUER.
This story is the best known and best loved work of the author.

Johanna Spyri's HEIDI. Illustrated by VINCENT O. COHEN.
This is the famous story of a Swiss child and her life among the Alps.

Charles Kingsley's THE HEROES. Illustrated by KIDDELL-MONROE.
A retelling of the legends of Perseus, the Argonauts and Theseus.

Louisa M. Alcott's JO'S BOYS. Illustrated by HARRY TOOTHILL.
'There is an abiding charm about the story.' *Scotsman.*

A. M. Hadfield's KING ARTHUR AND THE ROUND TABLE. Illustrated by DONALD SETON CAMMELL.
The haunting world of the Round Table.

Charlotte M. Yonge's THE LITTLE DUKE. Illustrated by MICHAEL GODFREY.
The story of Richard the Fearless, Duke of Normandy from 942 to 996.

Frances Hodgson Burnett's LITTLE LORD FAUNTLEROY.
'The best version of the Cinderella story in a modern idiom that exists.'
MARGHANITA LASKI.

Louisa M. Alcott's LITTLE MEN. Illustrated by HARRY TOOTHILL.
Harry Toothill's drawings capture the liveliness of a young gentlemen's academy.

Louisa M. Alcott's LITTLE WOMEN. Illustrated by S. VAN ABBÉ.
S. van Abbé's drawings capture the vivacity and charm of the March family.

Mrs Ewing's LOB LIE-BY-THE-FIRE and THE STORY OF A SHORT LIFE.
Illustrated by RANDOLPH CALDECOTT ('Lob') and H. M. BROCK ('Short Life').
Two of Mrs Ewing's most charming stories.

MODERN FAIRY STORIES. Edited by ROGER LANCELYN GREEN. Illustrated by E. H. SHEPARD.
Original (not 'retold') fairy stories by thirteen authors of modern times.

Jean Ingelow's MOPSA THE FAIRY. Illustrated by DORA CURTIS.
A river journey leads to the realms of wonder.

NURSERY RHYMES. Collected and illustrated in two-colour line by A. H. WATSON.
A comprehensive book of nursery rhymes.

Carlo Collodi's PINOCCHIO. The Story of a Puppet. Illustrated by CHARLES FOLKARD.
The most enchanting story of a puppet ever written.

Andrew Lang's PRINCE PRIGIO and PRINCE RICARDO. Illustrated by D. J. WATKINS-PITCHFORD.
Two modern fairy tales, rich in romantic adventures.

George MacDonald's THE LOST PRINCESS
 THE PRINCESS AND CURDIE
 THE PRINCESS AND THE GOBLIN
The first two volumes illustrated by CHARLES FOLKARD, the third by D. J. WATKINS-PITCHFORD.

Carola Oman's ROBIN HOOD. Illustrated by S. VAN ABBÉ.
Carola Oman lends substance to the 'Prince of Outlaws'.

W. M. Thackeray's THE ROSE AND THE RING and Charles Dickens's THE MAGIC FISH-BONE.
Two children's stories, the first containing the author's illustrations, the latter containing PAUL HOGARTH'S work.

J. R. Wyss's THE SWISS FAMILY ROBINSON. Illustrated by CHARLES FOLKARD.
This is a new version by Audrey Clark of the popular classic.

Charles and Mary Lamb's TALES FROM SHAKESPEARE. Illustrated by ARTHUR RACKHAM.

TALES OF MAKE-BELIEVE. Edited by ROGER LANCELYN GREEN. Illustrated by HARRY TOOTHILL.
Charles Dickens, Rudyard Kipling, E. Nesbit, Thomas Hardy, E. V. Lucas, etc.

Nathaniel Hawthorne's TANGLEWOOD TALES. Illustrated by S. VAN ABBÉ.
This is a sequel to the famous *Wonder Book*.

Thomas Hughes's TOM BROWN'S SCHOOLDAYS. Illustrated by S. VAN ABBÉ.
'The best story of a boy's schooldays ever written.'

Charles Kingsley's THE WATER-BABIES. Illustrated by ROSALIE K. FRY.
The artist's drawings delicately interpret the fantastic beauty of the underwater world.

Nathaniel Hawthorne's A WONDER BOOK. Illustrated by S. VAN ABBÉ.
Hawthorne's famous *Wonder Book* recalls the immortal fables of antiquity.

Selma Lagerlöf's THE WONDERFUL ADVENTURES OF NILS. Illustrated by HANS BAUMHAUER.
Translated into most languages of the world, this Swedish tale of the boy who rode on the back of a young gander and flew northwards to find surprising adventures is a great favourite. (Not available in the U.S.A. in this edition.)
See also THE FURTHER ADVENTURES OF NILS.

A Selection of
Illustrated Classics for Older Readers

Jules Verne's AROUND THE WORLD IN EIGHTY DAYS. Illustrated by W. F. PHILLIPPS.
The new translation by Robert and Jacqueline Baldick demonstrates here Verne's lively story-telling genius better than ever before.

Jack London's THE CALL OF THE WILD. Illustrated by CHARLES PICKARD.
This story of a dog called Buck is unique for its penetration into the uncanny understanding and reactions of a wild creature to moments of extreme tension.

Jean Webster's DADDY-LONG-LEGS. Illustrated by HARRY FAIRBAIRN.
'An all-time favourite' and best-seller.

Cervantes's DON QUIXOTE. Illustrated by W. HEATH ROBINSON.
An edition suitably edited from the Cervantes original.

Jonathan Swift's GULLIVER'S TRAVELS. Illustrated by ARTHUR RACKHAM.
Gulliver's Travels is one of the great satires in the English language.

Oscar Wilde's THE HAPPY PRINCE AND OTHER STORIES. Illustrated by PEGGY FORTNUM.
Oscar Wilde had a happy way with the modern fairy story—which has pleased both critics and readers. Kings, queens, witches, mermaids and dwarfs, even sorcerers, are here, but the author makes *all* his characters intensely human.

Edith Nesbit's THE HOUSE OF ARDEN. Illustrated by CLARKE HUTTON.
Magic and reality have little dividing line in this story where the Arden children, in search of the family treasure to repair the fortunes of the Arden estate, find themselves spirited away in a moment to Tudor days, the Napoleonic wars and Cromwell's Commonwealth.

Mark Twain's THE PRINCE AND THE PAUPER. Illustrated by ROBERT HODGSON.
The tale of a London beggar boy who changed places with the young prince of the realm—and found it difficult to cope with matters of state.

Anthony Hope's THE PRISONER OF ZENDA. Illustrated by MICHAEL GODFREY.
The Ruritanian romance in which Rudolph Rassendyll saves the Elphbergs' throne.

Daniel Defoe's ROBINSON CRUSOE. Illustrated by J. AYTON SYMINGTON.
An illustrated version which matches Defoe's great adventure story.

Anthony Hope's RUPERT OF HENTZAU. Illustrated by MICHAEL GODFREY.
The enthralling sequel to *The Prisoner of Zenda*.

TEN TALES OF DETECTION. Edited by ROGER LANCELYN GREEN. Illustrated by IAN RIBBONS.
Conan Doyle's Sherlock Holmes and other famous detectives of fiction.

Mark Twain's TOM SAWYER
HUCKLEBERRY FINN
These two Twain classics are superbly illustrated by C. WALTER HODGES.

Ernest Thompson Seton's THE TRAIL OF THE SANDHILL STAG and Other Lives of the Hunted. Illustrated with drawings by the author and coloured frontispiece by RITA PARSONS.

Robert Louis Stevenson's TREASURE ISLAND. Illustrated by S. VAN ABBÉ.
Probably no other illustrator of this famous tale has portrayed so vividly the characters in a book that lives so long in a boy's imagination.

Jack London's WHITE FANG. Illustrated by CHARLES PICKARD.
The famous story of a wild creature, part dog, part wolf; and his treatment under brutal masters and one that showed him affection.

Frank L. Baum's THE WONDERFUL WIZARD OF OZ. Illustrated by B. S. BIRO.

Further volumes in preparation